The Gathering of Friends ⚜

When someone comes

to your home and sits at your table and breaks bread

with you, your relationship is forever changed.

Michelle Huxtable Alyse Christensen

Photography by Matt Christensen

www.thegatheringoffriends.com

The
Gathering
of Friends ⚜

is a registered trademark of Clarenden Woods, LLC.

The Gathering of Friends. Second Printing
Library of Congress Control Number: 2008931341
ISBN: 978-0-9816986-0-1

Second Printing
10 9 8 7 6 5 4 3 2

Editor in Chief: Abby Jane Taylor
Executive Editor: Michelle Huxtable
Graphic Design: Kristy Witt

Published by Clarenden Woods, LLC.

❧ Contents ❧

❧ Preface ❧

To women everywhere who are part of this grand sisterhood, who derive great pleasure from hearth and home, there is something wonderful about carefully preparing and sharing a meal with another.

Food is a love language. The Gathering of Friends will empower the reader with ideas of how to open your homes to entertain new neighbors and business associates, celebrate the great blessings of a new baby or an upcoming wedding, strengthen family bonds, and encourage new friendships.

The recipes in this book are tried and true, and presented in such a way that any novice can pull off a special breakfast brunch, dinner party, or any "Gathering of Friends."

Each meal is outlined with a complete menu, photographed with table dressings and place settings. Each recipe is simple and loved by all who have sampled it.

In an age when most people meet at a restaurant and parties are catered, we suggest an alternative. Our hope is that this book will inspire the reader with ideas of how to enhance relationships, establish traditions and celebrate life.

Michelle Huxtable ❧ *Alyse Christensen*

CHAPTER ONE

Evening Gathering

The day's labors are complete. . . and the magic of evening begins as
you create a gathering place for family and friends around the table.

Treat your family as friends and your friends as family…dining

together in a familial atmosphere enjoying the warmth of association,

the variety of menu, and the gentle comfort of sharing time together.

Sweet Bran Muffins ⚜

1¼ c. all purpose flour

1 tbsp. baking powder

2 c. all-bran cereal

¼ c. vegetable oil

1 c. sugar

½ tsp. salt

1¼ c. milk

1 egg

Stir together flour, sugar, baking powder and salt. Set aside.

Preheat oven to 400°. In a large mixing bowl, combine all-bran cereal and milk. Let stand about 2 minutes or until cereal softens. Add egg and oil. Stir well. Gently fold flour mixture, stirring only until moistened. Pour evenly into greased muffin tins. Bake at 400° for 18-20 minutes. Do not over bake.

Optional addition: blend one cube of melted butter, 1 c. brown sugar, ¼ c. flour, and ¾ c. chopped pecans. Place a generous spoonful on the bottom of the greased muffin tins before pouring the batter in, or sprinkle on top of the batter before baking.

Pomegranate Salad ⚜

1 head Chinese cabbage, shredded

2 med. pomegranates, seeded

¼ tsp. coarse black pepper

1 c. toasted slivered almonds

½ head iceberg lettuce, shredded

Combine all ingredients and toss evenly. Refrigerate before serving.

Dressing:

2 tbsp. hot chili sesame oil

⅓ c. rice vinegar

2 tbsp. water

1 tbsp. minced ginger

2 tbsp. ketchup

¼ c. soy sauce

⅓ c. sugar

2 tbsp. lemon juice

½ tsp. pepper

½ c. mayonnaise

Combine dressing ingredients in blender and purée, chill. Toss with salad just before serving.

Stuffed Pork Roast ⚜

½ c. butter

1 whole onion, chopped

1 bunch of green onions

2 lbs. mushrooms

3 c. seasoned bread crumbs

1 c. chicken broth

1 tsp. salt

1 tsp. pepper

olive oil

Preheat oven to 325°. Sauté onions for 3–4 minutes in butter, add mushrooms and sauté, add chicken broth and fold in breadcrumbs.

5-6 lbs. Pork tenderloin

Prepare pork roast tenderloin by opening and flatten in 9"x 13" pan. Brush with olive oil evenly on top and bottom. Lightly sprinkle with salt and pepper. Fill with stuffing, tie off in 3 places. Pack extra stuffing around roast, top with green onion and bake at 325° for 70 minutes. Slice and serve.

Seasoned Potato Wedges and Peas ⚜

| 8-10 potatoes (Yukon Gold) | 3 tbsp. olive oil | 2 c. snap peas | 2 tbsp. Seasoning Mix |

Cook potatoes for 8 minutes in microwave then slice into wedges (as seen in picture). Lightly fry in olive oil and sprinkle with seasoning mix. Sauté both sides until slightly crisp. Toss with snap peas and continue to fry for 1 minute, turning twice. Do not overcook. Peas should be crisp. Serve immediately.

Seasoning Mix ⚜

Blend together:

¼ c. sun dried tomatoes	1 c. kosher sea salt	½ c. dried rosemary
2 tsp. dried red chili .	2 tbsp. coarse pepper	½ tsp. dry mustard

And mix separately:

1 tsp. basil	1 tsp. lemon peel	2 tsp. soy oil

Preheat oven to 325°. Toss dry ingredients with the soy oil mix. Bake at 325° for 15 minutes on a cookie sheet. Store in an air-tight container to retain freshness.

Applesauce ⚜

Purchase your favorite brand of applesauce and prior to serving add a drop of red food coloring for flare. Or pour it into a dish and sprinkle with a dash of ground cinnamon.

Shortbread Recipe ⚜

| 1 c. butter | 1 c. brown sugar | 2 c. flour | ½ tsp. salt | ½ tsp. baking powder |

Preheat oven to 300°. Let butter soften at room temperature. By hand, gently cream together butter and brown sugar. Carefully fold sifted flour, salt and baking powder into the cream mixture, handling as little as possible. Dough will be crumbly, lightly press dough into small torte pans (2½ inch diameter). Bake at 300° for 15-18 minutes or until golden. Watch carefully, do not overbake.

Using a small scoop to create vanilla ice cream balls, roll them in coconut and freeze. Using a larger scoop, make chocolate ice cream balls and roll them in Score™ bits. Freeze. Melt 8 oz. semi-sweet chocolate chips in the microwave for 1-1½ min. or until creamy. Do not overheat. When ready to serve place two ice cream balls on each shortbread torte add a strawberry and top with a heaping tbsp. of melted chocolate.

Helpful hint: To thin chocolate add 1 tbsp. of corn oil to every 8 oz. of chocolate.

Floral Centerpiece ⚜

Using any container, begin with a clump of Red Freesia secured with an elastic. Place it in the middle of the container surrounded with green flower bells of Ireland. For added garnish place Hypericum berries throughout arrangement. Changing the water every couple of days will help flowers last 1½ to 2 weeks.

Shopping List

For 10-12 people

1 lemon	iceberg lettuce	vegetable oil	applesauce
1 onion	5-6 lbs. pork tenderloin	sesame oil	¼ c. sun-dried tomatoes
1 bunch green onions	All-Bran cereal	soy oil	dried red chilies
2 lbs. mushrooms	bread crumbs	corn oil	dried rosemary
8-10 yellow potatoes	dried coconut for baking	rice vinegar	ginger
2 c. snap peas	Score bits (toffee bits)	slivered almonds	vanilla ice cream
pomegranates	mustard	kosher sea salt	chocolate ice cream
strawberries	dried basil	coarse pepper	ketchup
Chinese cabbage	nutmeg	1 c. chicken broth	mayonnaise

Staples:

	milk	baking powder	pepper
	eggs	brown sugar	2 c. butter
	flour	sugar	olive oil
	baking soda	salt	

Notes

Date of Gathering: _____

Guest List: _____

_____

Date of Gathering: _____

Guest List: _____

_____

Date of Gathering: _____

Guest List: _____

_____

Date of Gathering: _____

Guest List: _____

_____

Date of Gathering: _____

Guest List: _____

_____

Comments

_____
_____
_____
_____
_____
_____
_____
_____
_____
_____
_____
_____

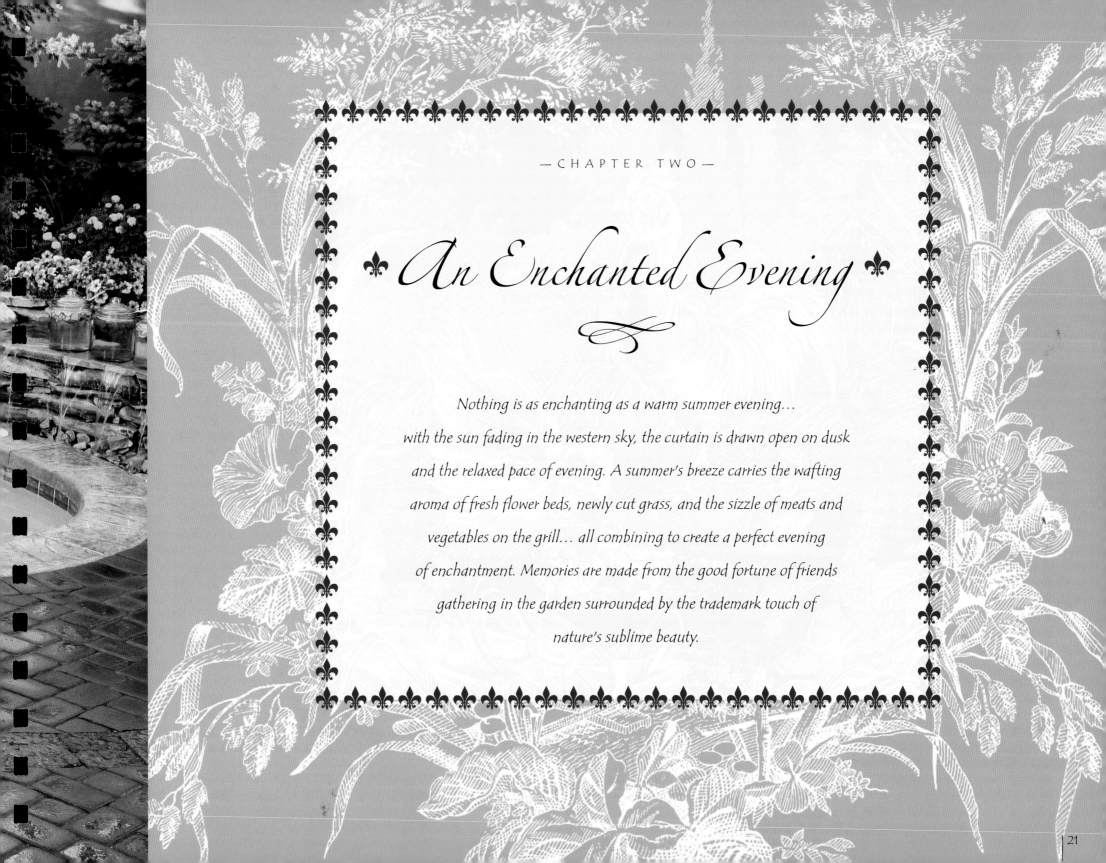

—CHAPTER TWO—

❦ An Enchanted Evening ❦

Nothing is as enchanting as a warm summer evening…

with the sun fading in the western sky, the curtain is drawn open on dusk

and the relaxed pace of evening. A summer's breeze carries the wafting

aroma of fresh flower beds, newly cut grass, and the sizzle of meats and

vegetables on the grill… all combining to create a perfect evening

of enchantment. Memories are made from the good fortune of friends

gathering in the garden surrounded by the trademark touch of

nature's sublime beauty.

Zesty Grilled Chicken ⚜

12 chicken breasts

16 oz. 7up™ soda

16 oz. Kraft Zesty Italian™ salad dressing

Combine equal parts of 7up™ and Italian dressing in heavy ziplock bag. Place chicken breasts in marinade, cover chicken completely. Marinate overnight if possible. Grill on medium heat for 14-16 minutes, turning twice.

Lemon Pepper Salmon ⚜

2 large salmon filets   ¼ c. melted butter   lemon pepper

Using two sheets of tinfoil, make a tent enclosing the filets. Brush the salmon with butter and sprinkle with lemon pepper. Tightly seal the foil to hold in juices.

Grill for 30-35 minutes on medium heat. Or bake at 350° for 45-50 minutes. Garnish with fresh parsley.

Grilled Asparagus ⚜

2 bunches asparagus   2 tbsp. olive oil

lemon pepper to taste

Cut off the end 2 inches of the asparagus where it is tough. Rinse with water. Brush with olive oil and season with salt and pepper or lemon pepper. Place on the grill for 15-20 minutes or until tender, turning occasionally.

Grilled Sweet Potatoes ⚜

4 large sweet potatoes   2 tbsp. olive oil

2 tsp. kosher sea salt

Peel and cut sweet potatoes into julienned slices. Rub with olive oil and kosher sea salt. Grill on medium heat for 15-20 minutes, turning occasionally. Serve immediately.

Croissant Parmesan Twists ⚜

½ c. water

½ c. evaporated milk

3 tbsp. butter, room temperature

1 egg, room temperature

1½ tsp. salt

3 tbsp. sugar

3 c. bread flour

2¼ tsp. active dry yeast

Parmesan Finish

1 tbsp. water

1 egg, beaten

1 c. Parmesan cheese

Combine dry mixture, liquid ingredients, and butter in mixing bowl on low speed. Beat 2 to 3 minutes on medium speed. Add egg; beat 1 minute. By hand, stir in enough remaining flour to make firm dough. Knead on floured surface 5 to 7 minutes or until smooth and elastic. Use additional flour if necessary.

Preheat oven to 350°. Place dough in lightly oiled bowl and turn to grease top. Cover and refrigerate for 2 hours. Place dough on floured surface and knead about 6 times to release air bubbles. Divide into 3 parts. Roll each part into a rectangular shape. With a sharp knife, cut into long strips, 1½ inch wide. Twist strips and place on ungreased cookie sheets. Cover; let rise until indentation remains after touching. Combine 1 slightly beaten egg and 1 tbsp. water; brush croissants with egg mixture and sprinkle with Parmesan cheese. Bake at 350° for 11 to 15 minutes or until golden brown. Remove from cookie sheets and cool.

Couscous Shrimp Salad ⚜

A green salad with ranch dressing is perfect for all kids, and some husbands. We love to prepare this couscous shrimp salad to add to any green salad with this spicy dressing. You will love it. It could be a meal all on its own!

2 c. boiling water   2 c. couscous   2 tsp. butter
1 ½ tsp. granulated chicken bouillon

Stir couscous into boiling water. Blend in butter and bouillon, cover and set aside. Ready in five minutes.

Combine:
1 red bell pepper, diced
1 yellow bell pepper, diced
1 lb. green beans, cut into ¼ inch chunks,
   blanched and set aside
12 oz. bag frozen white corn
2 lbs. cooked bay shrimp, rinsed and set aside
¾ c. cilantro, minced

Combine couscous and vegetables with shrimp and toss. Arrange couscous salad on green salad. Top with dressing.

Spicy Ranch Dressing:

1 ranch dressing packet
1 c. milk
1 c. mayonnaise
2 fresh jalapeños, minced
1 tbsp. ketchup
1 tbsp. Worcestershire sauce
½ tsp. pepper

Wisk together milk, mayo, and dressing packet. Fold in remaining ingredients and chill.

Chocolate Fountain Dessert Table ⚜

Follow directions carefully for melting and thinning chocolate. If it is too thick, the chocolate will clog the fountain and it won't run like it should. You can serve it with any of your favorite treats cut into small, bite-size pieces. Ideas include: Bananas, brownies, macaroons, pound cake, pretzels, Rice Krispie Treats™, strawberries, etc.

Decorative Water Jars ⚜

Simply fill desired glass jar with water. You may combine your favorite fruit or vegetable in glass jar depending on desired color or flavor. Options include strawberries, sliced lemons, cucumbers or limes. Wash fruit or vegetables thoroughly, before placing in jars.

Artichoke and ⚜ Candle Clay Pot

Using an artificial artichoke we opened up the leaves and placed a candle in the center. Set into a terracotta pot filled with styrofoam, we then filled around the base with artificial moss. Tied with a bow, this made a delightful accent for this enchanted evening.

❧ Shopping List ❧

For 10-12 people

2 hearts of Romaine lettuce heads	2 lbs. bay shrimp	bite size treats (Rice Krispy Treats™,
2 English cucumber	Parmesan cheese	brownie bites, pretzels, bananas,
½ lb. cherry tomatoes	lemon pepper	strawberries, pineapple, and
1 lb. bacon	evaporated milk	coconut macaroons)
celery	bread flour	chocolate for fondue
cilantro	couscous	cucumbers, strawberries,
red and yellow bell peppers	active dry yeast	lemons for water jugs
green beans	2 large salmon filets	
4 large sweet potatoes	12 chicken breasts	
2 bunches asparagus	16 oz. 7up™ soda	
frozen white corn	Italian dressing mix	

Staples:

	egg	salt
	sugar	2 c. butter

❧ Notes ❧

Date of Gathering: _____

Guest List: _____

_____

Date of Gathering: _____

Guest List: _____

_____

Date of Gathering: _____

Guest List: _____

_____

Date of Gathering: _____

Guest List: _____

_____

Date of Gathering: _____

Guest List: _____

_____

✤ Comments ✤

_____

_____

_____

_____

_____

_____

_____

_____

_____

_____

_____

_____

CHAPTER THREE

Supper with Friends

Isn't it magical, after a long Indian summer, the rustle of autumn

leaves signals the season of harvest… and as daylight diminishes

and temperatures cool, we retreat indoors intrigued by tempting

tastes of comfort foods— soups and chili, warm breads and pies.

Here is a simple yet elegant meal that everyone will wish for

long after sharing supper at your table.

Tomato & Rice Supreme ⚜

1-26 oz. jar of Tomato & Basil Classico® Traditional Favorite Pasta Sauce

26 oz. whipping cream (optional substitution: half and half)

½ c. sugar

1½ tsp. Worcestershire sauce

salt and pepper to taste

4 c. sticky rice

Purée pasta sauce in blender. Combine sauce and cream in heavy pot. Fold in sugar, Worcestershire sauce, and salt and pepper to taste. Heat thoroughly (do not to bring to a boil). Using a heart shape measuring cup, or ice cream scoop place rice ball in center of the bowl of soup. Top with ground pepper. *Helpful hint: As a time saver stop by your favorite Chinese food restaurant and purchase a cartoon of sticky rice.*

Parmesan Toast ⚜

½ c. mayonnaise

½ c. butter

½ c. Parmesan cheese

1 baguette or loaf of French bread

Slice bread to desired thickness. Blend mayo, butter and Parmesan cheese. Spread on bread slices. Broil till golden.

Spicy Sauce ⚜

1 c. corn syrup

½ c. rice vinegar

½ tbsp. dark sesame oil

3 tbsp. peanut butter

½ crushed red chili pepper

⅓ c. soy sauce.

Bring ingredients to a boil and cook for 3-4 minutes. Place spoonfuls of meat on lettuce leaves and pour heated sauce over them to serve.

Asian Style Lettuce Wraps ⚜

2 hearts of Romaine lettuce heads

2 tsp. toasted sesame oil

2 lbs. of ground sausage
  or spicy Italian pork (preference)

¼ head purple cabbage shredded

½ head cabbage shredded

Place oil in skillet, sauté ground sausage, stirring continually as sausage cooks. As sausage browns combine shredded cabbages and cook for additional 2-3 minutes. Turn off heat and cover with lid to keep warm, serve immediately.

Apple Chicken Crunch ❧

3 lbs. chicken tenders

1½ c. dried cranberries

1½ c. chopped walnuts

2 c. apples, peeled and cubed small

salt and pepper to taste

1 package lettuce hearts, cleaned and dried

Dressing:

1 medium red onion

1 c. sugar

1 c. oil

2 tsp. dry mustard powder

2 c. red wine vinegar

½ tsp. salt

½ tsp. pepper

Place frozen chicken tenders in a heavy pot with lid. Cook for 12-15 minutes on medium heat. Drain and cool chicken. Cut in bite size pieces. Combine the cranberries, walnuts and apple chunks with chicken.

Purée dressing ingredients in a blender. Toss chicken mixture together with desired amount of dressing and Chill.

Clean the lettuce hearts and dry them. Place in fridge until crisp. Serve them separately so your guests can help themselves.

French Mint ⚜

2 c. butter

4 c. powdered sugar

8 oz. dark sweetened chocolate squares, melted

8 eggs, added one at a time

½ tsp. mint extract

2 c. chopped pecans, or your favorite nut, optional

Place softened butter and powdered sugar in mix master and beat on high for 15 minutes. Combine cooled chocolate to butter mixture and beat on high for 5 minutes. Add eggs one at a time mixing thoroughly after each egg. Fold in mint extract. Using a spring form pan line bottom of the pan with pecans. Pour chocolate mixture in pan. You may also use cupcake foils or cupcake tins for a perfect size serving. Allow 3 hours before serving. Place in the freezer until set up.

*If mint is not your favorite, substitute ½ tsp. almond or vanilla extract, or omit extracts completely for a rich chocolate treat!

Table Scape ⚜

We have used three small antique creamers and two large Spode™ teacups and saucers. This set up takes 4 dozen roses with the stems cut short for desired height add small bunches of Hypericum coffee (or green) Ivy Flair. When bunching them together put an elastic around the stems so they hold their shape, just make sure to change the water every other day and they will last beautifully for weeks.

❧ *Shopping List* ❧

For 10-12 people

1 red onion	Tomato & Basil Classico™ sauce	toasted sesame oil	corn syrup
2 large apples	sticky rice	rice vinegar	powdered sugar
3 heads of Romaine lettuce	mayonnaise	crushed red chili pepper	dark sweetened chocolate
¼ head purple cabbage	dry mustard powder	soy sauce	mint extract
½ head cabbage	red wine vinegar	dark sesame oil	pecans
heavy whipping cream	3 lbs. chicken tenders	Craisins™	baguette
Parmesan cheese	2 lbs. ground sausage	walnuts	
Worcestershire sauce	or spicy Italian	peanut butter	

Staples:	sugar	pepper	4 c. butter
	salt	vegetable oil	

❦ Notes ❦

Date of Gathering:_____

Guest List:_____

_____

Date of Gathering:_____

Guest List:_____

_____

Date of Gathering:_____

Guest List:_____

_____

Date of Gathering:_____

Guest List:_____

_____

Date of Gathering:_____

Guest List:_____

_____

Place Settings ❧ We love to collect antique dishes. While traveling it's fun to find unique and different place settings… any old style will work. Soup served with lettuce wraps are the perfect combination to please everyone. Borrowing place settings from family and friends can help create a unique table setting.

CHAPTER FOUR

❧ *Romantic Repast* ❧

Celebrate any evening sharing in love an exquisite dinner by the soft glimmer of flickering candles and the harmony of hearts warmed by an unforgettable mood. No need to wait for an anniversary, birthday, or other special occasion. The intensity of a busy week will quickly fade in the romantic quietude of an evening gathering. Everything always tastes better by candlelight.

Romantic Evening Salad ⚜

The Wedge:

Cut Iceberg lettuce into wedge slices

1 c. cherry tomatoes

Dressing:

½ lb. Roquefort cheese crumbled

1 c. mayonnaise

1 c. whipping cream or milk

½ tsp. coarse black pepper

2 tbsp. lemon juice

1 tsp. garlic saltt

Blend all ingredients together and pour over wedge

Cinnamon Raisin Bread ⚜

3½ c. flour

¼ tsp. instant yeast

1¼ tsp. salt

1½ c. water

½ c. sugar

¾ c. raisins

2 tsp. cinnamon

1 tsp. nutmeg

Mix all ingredients with a spoon. Let rest for 11-16 hours (bubbles will form on top).

Roughly fold into loaf in the shape of a hub cap. Let rise for 1½- 2 hours on wax paper.

Preheat oven and cast iron pan at 450°.v Flip bread into dish, cover and bake for 30 minutes. Take lid off and bake for another 15 minutes.

Brush with virgin olive oil and then sprinkle with seasoning.

Salmon and Asparagus Pasta ⚜

White Wine Lemon Sauce:

½ c. butter	½ c. Parmesan cheese
1 tsp. Granulated chicken bouillon	¾ tsp. pepper
⅓ c. flour	4 tbsp. lemon rind
3 c. cream	½ c. white wine

Sauce preparation:

Sauté butter in skillet adding granulated chicken bouillon, flour and pepper. Stirring constantly scorch the mixture until it is golden brown. Slowly fold in the cream, Parmesan cheese , 2 tbsp. lemon rind and white wine. Simmer 3-4 minutes.

---

2 large salmon fillets	lemon pepper	16 oz. package angel hair pasta	2 bunches asparagus with ends clipped

---

Preheat oven to 325°. Place Salmon fillets on aluminum foil and place on a baking sheet. Brush the fillets with butter and cover in lemon pepper. Seal the foil and bake in the oven for 35 minutes.

Bring water, olive oil, and salt to a boil. Cook the angel hair pasta as per instructions. Do not over cook. Cut off ends of asparagus and blanch for 1½ minutes.

Food Presentation:

Place asparagus on plate, add angel hair pasta, and broken pieces of salmon. Drizzle with cream sauce and finish with fresh ground pepper, grated fresh lemon rind, toped with parsley sprig. Ready to serve.

Strawberry Cream Puffs ❖

½ c. butter

1 c. boiling water

1 c. all-purpose flour, sifted

¼ tsp. salt

4 eggs

Preheat oven to 400°. Place butter in 1 c. boiling water. As butter melts, fold in flour and salt. Stir vigorously. Continue to stir till mixture forms a ball that doesn't separate. Remove from heat; cool slightly. Add eggs, one at a time, beating after each until smooth.

Place on greased cookie sheet in heaping tablespoons 3 inches apart (or desired size). Bake at 400° for 30min. or until golden brown and puffy, Remove from oven; slice in half. Cool.

strawberries and chocolate—also delicious: bananas and vanilla pudding, chocolate pudding, or any combination of fruit, pudding and cream

Filling and topping:

    1 pint heavy cream

    1 tsp. vanilla

    ½ to ¾ c. sugar (to taste)

    12 oz. chocolate chips

    2 c. strawberries

Whip heavy cream until stiff, fold in ½ to ¾ c. sugar and vanilla. Open cream puffs, spread whip cream and top with strawberries. Replace top portion of cream puff. Melt chocolate chips in microwave for 1 minute or until smooth. Be careful not to overheat. Spread over each cream puff and refrigerate.

Floral Centerpiece ⚜ This look can be accomplished with roses in any color. Just clip to fit tightly into the vase of choice. This container is clear and is filled with glass beads to enhance the look.

Shopping List

For 10-12 people

2 lemons	white cooking wine	granulated chicken bouillon
2 heads iceberg lettuce	Parmesan cheese	16 oz. package angel hair pasta
1 c. cherry tomatoes	instant yeast	2 large salmon fillets
2 bunches asparagus	heavy whipping cream	nutmeg
½ lb. roquefort cheese	raisins	
mayonnaise	chocolate chips	

Staples:	flour	eggs
	salt sugar	vanilla
	course pepper	cinnamon
	butter	milk

Notes

Date of Gathering: _____

Guest List: _____

_____

Date of Gathering: _____

Guest List: _____

_____

Date of Gathering: _____

Guest List: _____

_____

Date of Gathering: _____

Guest List: _____

_____

Date of Gathering: _____

Guest List: _____

_____

❧ Comments ❧

—CHAPTER FIVE—

❧ Autumn Gathering ❧

Remember the last time you were invited to someone's home for an intimate

gathering? Your guests will be as pleased as you felt when you suggest

gathering in your home. Gracious hosting and a kind manner conveys to

others how important they are to you. The time you spend planning and

preparing a meal for friends to enjoy creates opportunity for engaging conversation

and is the sparkle of friendship. Let's make food your love language.

Carrot Puffs ⚜

1 lb. carrots

¾ to 1 c. milk

3 eggs, beaten

½ c. sugar

2 tbsp. flour

1 tbsp. baking powder

¼ tsp. cinnamon

½ c. butter, melted

4 oz. cream cheese

Preheat oven to 350°. Cut carrots in one inch pieces, sauté in saucepan until tender; drain. Mix carrots with milk in a food processor until smooth. Combine in bowl, eggs, sugar, flour, baking powder, and cinnamon, mix well. Fold in butter and mix lightly. Spoon into a 1 to 1½ quart baking dish. (we have used muffin tins) Bake at 350° for 30 minutes or until the center is set and springs back when lightly touched. Garnish with a dollop of whipped cream cheese.

Fall Salad ⚜

1 head red leaf lettuce

2 heads hearts of romaine

2 c. glazed pecans

12 oz. blue-cheese

¼ tsp. cayenne pepper

2 tbsp. water

1 pkg. Italian dry package dressing

1 red onion, diced

1 red pepper, diced

3 cloves garlic

1 c. yellow raisins

¼ c. sugar

Prepare glazed nuts by placing pecans, sugar, and water in saucepan. Cook for 4-5 minutes or until sugar lightly boils. Pour onto a cookie sheet, let cool. Prepare Italian dressing as directed, but replace vinegar with Balsamic vinegar; add garlic, and cayenne pepper. Crumble blue-cheese and toss with remaining ingredients. Top with dressing just before serving.

Focaccia Bread ⚜

2¾ c. all-purpose flour

1 tsp. salt

1 tsp. white sugar

1 tbsp. active dry yeast

1 tbsp. vegetable oil

1 c. water

1 tsp. garlic powder

1-2 tbsp. olive oil

1 tsp. dried oregano

1 tsp. dried thyme

1 tsp. fresh minced basil

1 pinch ground black pepper

3 tbsp. grated Parmesan cheese

1 c. mozzarella

In a large bowl, place flour, salt, sugar, yeast, and garlic powder. Fold in the vegetable oil and water. When the dough has come together, place it on a lightly floured surface, and knead it until resilient but smooth. Lightly brush with oil on both sides and place the dough in the bowl. Cover with a damp cloth, and let rise in a warm place for 20 minutes.

Preheat oven to 450°. Press dough down and flatten; place on greased baking sheet. Pat into a ½ inch thick rectangle. Brush top with olive oil and sprinkle with final ingredients of oregano, thyme, basil, black pepper, Parmesan cheese and mozzarella cheese. Bake in preheated oven for 15 minutes, or until golden brown. Serve warm.

Rice Pilaf ❖

2 tsp. Granulated chicken bullion

1 c. brown rice

8 oz. pkg. shredded carrots

1 bundle of green onions

1 tsp. sea salt

1 c. white rice

Cook both kinds of rice according to directions, add 1 tsp. bouillon for each cup of rice. Prepare rice separately, fold in the grated carrots and green onions just before serving.

Beef Tenderloin with Crab ❖

| 3 lbs. beef tenderloin | 1 lb. fresh, uncooked crab | olive oil |

Preheat oven to 425°. Carve tenderloin into ¼ inch thick slices. Stuff each slice with fresh uncooked crab. As you roll the tenderloin, secure it with a toothpick. Line a cookie sheet with the tenderloins, brush lightly with olive oil and sea salt. Cook on 425° for 15 minutes. Garnish with fresh rosemary. Serve immediately.

Peach Cheesecake Puffs ⚜

1 (17 oz.) pkg. frozen puff pastry

6 ripe peaches

8 oz. cream cheese

7 oz. sweetened condensed milk

1 pint heavy whipping cream

½ to ¾ c. sugar

2 tsp. fresh lemon juice

1 tsp. vanilla

Cut frozen puff pastry into 2½ to 3 inch squares before baking. Place on cooking sheet 1 inch apart and bake according to directions on package.

Whip cream by beating one pint of heavy cream until stiff, fold in ½ to ¾ c. sugar (or to taste) and 1 tsp. vanilla. In a separate bowl, blend together cream cheese and sweetened condensed milk until smooth. Fold in lemon juice and chill.

Separate pastry sheets (cut the top part off as it will become a lid). Spread cheese filling and sliced peaches. Top with whipped cream and place lid on top with a small dollop of whipped cream.

Centerpiece Floral Arrangement Four heads of flowering Kale leaves are held together with an elastic, and then surrounded by yellow Freesia. Flowers such as Baby's Breath are then added for bulk, variety and texture.

⚜ *Shopping List* ⚜

For 10-12 people

1 head red leaf lettuce	fresh parsley	Italian dressing mix	17 oz. package frozen
2 heads hearts of Romaine	12 oz. crumbled blue cheese	white rice	puff pastry
1 bundle green onions	4 oz. mozzarella cheese	brown rice	heavy whipping cream
1 lb. carrots	12 oz. cream cheese	garlic powder	sweetened condensed milk
8 oz. shredded carrots	1 lb. fresh uncooked crab	2 c. whole pecans	Parmesan cheese
6 ripe peaches	3 lbs. beef tenderloin	red pepper	fresh basil
2 red onions	granulated chicken bouillon	yellow raisins	active dry yeast
fresh garlic	balsamic vinegar	fresh rosemary	lemon juice

Staples:	olive oil	sugar	vanilla
	vegetable oil	flour	thyme
	sea salt	baking powder	oregano
	milk	cinnamon	cayenne pepper
	eggs	butter	

Notes

Date of Gathering: _____

Guest List: _____

_____

Date of Gathering: _____

Guest List: _____

_____

Date of Gathering: _____

Guest List: _____

_____

Date of Gathering: _____

Guest List: _____

_____

Date of Gathering: _____

Guest List: _____

_____

❧ Comments ❧

_____
_____
_____
_____
_____
_____
_____
_____
_____
_____
_____
_____

CHAPTER SIX

A Christmas
Celebration

Moments when memories are made... there is enduring value in holiday traditions when family and friends gather to celebrate. At the center of every gathering a meal is shared with those who have traveled near and far. The feast can be an expression of love where thoughtful menu selection appeals to the appetite of any age. Here is a holiday feast that can be prepared on any scale— be it intimate or grand. Every guest will enjoy the bounty of a generous meal in a festive mood of merriment and the bright cheer of happy hearts.

Shrimp Salad ⚜

2 heads Romaine lettuce   3 avocados, sliced   2 lbs. baby shrimp, cleaned and cooked

¼ lb. grape tomatoes   fresh ground pepper

Rinse, dry and break hearts of romaine into bite-size pieces. Place in serving bowl. Add sliced avocados, tomatoes, and shrimp. Top with cracked pepper. Serve with our Traditional Thousand Island Dressing.

Traditional Thousand
Island Dressing:

2 c. mayonnaise

½ c. milk

½ c. ketchup

1 c. cocktail sauce

1 c. butter pickles, minced

1 tsp. Worcestershire sauce

1 tsp. coarse, dry pepper

Blend all ingredients well
and refrigerate until ready
to serve.

Steamed Asparagus with Bacon ⚜

3 bundles of asparagus

1 lb. bacon

Rinse asparagus and cut off the last 2 inches. Blanche for 2 minutes (careful not to overcook). Sauté bacon, cut in small pieces in frying pan until crisp, stirring occasionally (set aside bacon grease for baby reds pg.67) Arrange asparagus in serving dish and sprinkle with warm bacon pieces, serve.

Feta Salad ⚜

Combine:

½ lb. grape tomatoes	1 avocado, cubed	1 c. black olives, sliced
2 c. marinated artichoke hearts	2 c. jicama, cubed	1 c. feta cheese, crumbled

Balsamic Dressing:

¾ c. olive oil	1 shallot, finely chopped	¼ c. Balsamic vinegar
¼ tsp. salt	¼ tsp. fresh ground pepper	

Mix dressing ingredients and toss with salad. Sprinkle with feta cheese. Chill until ready to serve.

Flank Steak ⚜

Marinade:

1 c. onion, minced	1 tbsp. ginger
½ c. oil	½ c. soy sauce
1 c. honey	½ tsp. salt
½ c. vinegar	½ tsp. pepper

4-5 lbs. flank steak

When purchasing flank steak, ask the grocer, to run it through the tenderizer twice. Mix all marinade ingredients together and put the steak in a ziplock bag. Marinade for 2 days, rotate if possible. Grill on medium for 15 minutes, turning once or twice. Cut on diagonal into thin strips and serve.

Baby Reds ⚜

1 lb. bacon

8 lbs. baby red potatoes

½ c. cilantro, chopped

Preheat oven to 375°. Dice bacon and sauté, separate grease and set aside. Slice potatoes in half. Toss potatoes in bacon grease, then place face down on a cookie sheet and bake at 375° Potatoes will fry when placed face down. Cook for 1 hour. Toss with cilantro and serve. (bacon pieces to be used with steamed asparagus. pg.65)

Heavenly Rolls ⚜

1 envelope active dry yeast

¼ c. warm water

⅓ c. sugar

½ c. butter

2 tsp. salt

1 c. scalding hot milk

1 egg, lightly beaten

4½ c. sifted all-purpose flour

Sprinkle yeast into a large bowl with very warm water. Stir until yeast dissolves. Combine sugar, butter and salt with hot milk and stir until the sugar dissolves and the butter is melted. Cool mixture to 105° to 115°. Add milk mixture to yeast, and beat in egg. Beat in 4 cups of flour, 1 cup at a time, to form a soft dough. Use some of the remaining ½ cup of flour to dust a pastry cloth. Knead the dough lightly for 5 minutes, working in the remaining flour (use it for flouring the pastry cloth and your hands). Place dough in a warm buttered bowl; turn greased side up. Cover and let rise in a warm place until doubled in bulk, about 90 minutes.

Preheat oven to 375°. Punch dough down and knead 4 to 5 minutes on a lightly floured pastry cloth. Dough will be sticky, but use as little flour as possible for flouring your hands and the pastry cloth. Take off small chunks of dough and shape into round rolls about 1½ inch in diameter. Place in neat rows, not quite touching, on a well-greased cookie sheet. Cover rolls and let rise in a warm place until doubled in bulk, 30 to 40 minutes. Brush tops of rolls with melted butter, and bake at 375° for 18 to 20 minutes or until nicely browned. Serve warm with plenty of butter.

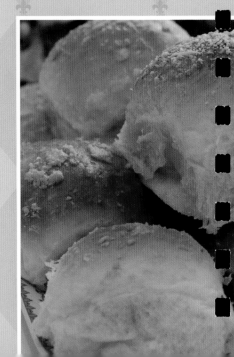

Honey Butter ⚜

1 c. butter, softened

1 c. honey

Whip until creamy and serve.

Raspberry Butter ⚜

1 c. butter, softened

2 c. fresh raspberries, or you can substitute
your favorite raspberry jam

Whip until creamy and serve.

Helpful Hint: Buy any brand of frozen dinner rolls. Roll them in warm butter and Parmesan cheese. Place on greased baking sheet. Let rise and bake according to the directions on the package.

Peppermint Cake ⚜

1 angel food cake
   (You can make one or pick one up at
   your neighborhood grocer)
2 c. whipping cream
½ c. sugar
2 tsp. vanilla
1 c. crushed candy canes

In a chilled bowl whip the cream until stiff
peaks appear, fold in sugar and vanilla.
Frost the cake and sprinkle with crushed
candy canes.

*Helpful Hint: Sprinkle crushed candy cane
just before serving or it will dissolve.*

Chocolate Angel Food Cake ⚜

1 angel food cake

(You can make one or pick one up at your
neighborhood grocer)

2 c. whipping cream

1 (5 oz.) chocolate instant pudding mix

¼ c. sugar

2 tsp. vanilla

1 chocolate Hershey™ bar, grated

In a chilled bowl whip the cream until stiff peaks appear,
add sugar, vanilla, fold in pudding mix. It will thicken
quickly. (You can add a little milk to thin the consistency
if needed.) Frost the cake and sprinkle it with chocolate
shavings. *Option: Sprinkle with Skor™ bar.*

White Rose and ⚜ Cranberry Centerpiece

Fill your desired vase or glass container with cranberries. Add water. Cut and arrange white roses tightly together. Tie with your favorite ribbon.

Shopping List

For 10-12 people

2 heads Romaine lettuce	1 shallot	ketchup	4 c. heavy whipping cream
3 bundles asparagus	8 oz. feta cheese	Worcestershire sauce	5 oz. chocolate pudding mix
16 oz. fresh raspberries	1 lb. bacon	2 c. honey	2 angel food cakes
4 avocados	2 lbs. baby shrimp	vinegar	chocolate bar
¾ lb. grape tomatoes	4–5 lbs. flank steak	balsamic vinegar	peppermint candy canes
8 lbs. baby red potatoes	2 c. marinated artichoke hearts	ginger powder	2 lbs. butter
1–2 large onion	butter pickles	yeast packets	
fresh cilantro	black olives	soy sauce	
2 c. jicama	mayonnaise	1 c. cocktail sauce	

Staples:			
	milk	pepper	eggs
	vegetable oil	sugar	vanilla
	salt	flour	olive oil

Notes

Date of Gathering: _____

Guest List: _____

_____

Date of Gathering: _____

Guest List: _____

_____

Date of Gathering: _____

Guest List: _____

_____

Date of Gathering: _____

Guest List: _____

_____

Date of Gathering: _____

Guest List: _____

_____

❦ Comments ❦

CHAPTER SEVEN

Treats
❧ And Tokens ❧

The kind gesture of arriving as a guest with a token of appreciation

is long remembered by the hostess and to the delight of others. Each

of these recipes are fun as entertaining treats you make for your

party or they can be wrapped with a bow and taken as a gift.

Treats and Tokens are easy to make and a joy to share.

Spiced Nuts ⚜

1 c. sugar

⅓ c. boiling water

½ tsp. vanilla

1 tsp. Karo™ syrup

2 c. whole nuts (walnuts, pecans,
   almonds, etc.)

½ tsp. cinnamon

¼ tsp. salt

¼ tsp ginger

½ tsp. cloves

Combine sugar, water, syrup, salt, and spices,
bringing to a boil until syrup spins a short
thread. Remove from heat. Add vanilla and
nuts. Stir until mixture sugars. Turn onto a
flat surface and separate the nuts. Spread out
on wax paper.

Roasted Rosemary Cashews ⚜

1 lb. of raw cashews (not roasted)

½ tsp. cayenne pepper

1 tsp. Kosher salt

2 tbsp. minced fresh rosemary

2 tsp. brown sugar

1 tbsp. unsalted butter

Preheat oven to 350°. Combine ingredients and toss with nuts. Bake cashews
at 350° on cookie sheet for 5-7 minutes. Serve warm.

Caramel Dip ⚜

½ c. butter   2 c. brown sugar

1 c. light corn syrup   1 tsp. vanilla

14 oz. can sweetened condensed milk

In saucepan, combine butter, sugar, and corn syrup. Stir well and bring to a boil over medium heat. Stir in condensed milk, simmer, stirring constantly, until caramel forms a soft ball when dropped into cold water. Stir in vanilla. Heat to serve.

Great for making caramel popcorn!

Hot Fudge ⚜

½ c. butter

1 12 oz. can evaporated milk

2½ sq. unsweetened chocolate

3 c. powdered sugar

1½ tsp. vanilla

In a double broiler melt butter and chocolate. Add milk and powdered sugar stirring constantly on low heat until it comes to a boil. Boil on low approximately 8 minutes until thick. Fold in vanilla and stir until creamy. Pour in glass container and serve over ice cream.

White Chocolate Popcorn with Peppermint ⚜

10 c. popped and buttered popcorn

24 oz. white chocolate chips

A dash of salt

2 candy canes, crushed (optional)

Pour popped popcorn in large bowl, add a dash of salt and set aside. Melt white chocolate slowly in the microwave stirring every 30 seconds until smooth (a minute to a minute and a half). Spread popcorn out on a cookie sheet. Drizzle warm chocolate over popcorn until evenly coated. Add crushed candy cane if desired, let cool.

Shrimp Dip ⚜

8 oz. cream cheese   1 can devained bay shrimp

5 oz. can evaporated milk   dash onion salt

dash garlic powder

Warm cream cheese and add shrimp. Stir in evaporated milk and season with onion salt and garlic powder. This is a favorite family recipe. Serve with Ruffles™ or your favorite vegetable.

Relish Appetizer ⚜

| 8 oz. of cream cheese | 1 jar of Harry & David, Pepper & Onion Relish™ | 1 can corn |
| ¼ c. diced red peppers | 2 tsp. dried chili peppers | 3 green onions. |

Place cream cheese on a platter. Top with 1 jar of Harry & David Pepper & Onion Relish™, mixed with corn and peppers. Topped with diced green onions. Serve with rice crackers, Wheat Thins™ or your favorite cracker.

Homemade Granola ⚜

1½ c. brown sugar   ½ c. honey   2 tsp. cinnamon   ½ c. dark molasses

1½ tsp. salt   3 tsp. vanilla   1½ c. water   ½ c. butter

Combine all ingredients and bring to a boil. Set aside.

Combine:

    10 c. oats

    4 large shredded wheat biscuits, broken

    2 heaping c. of big shredded coconut

    ½ c. sesame seeds

    2 c. pumpkin seeds

    2 c. sunflower seeds

    2 c. whole almonds

Preheat oven to 325°. Drizzle glaze over dry mixture and coat thoroughly. Spread over a cookie sheet and bake at 325° for 20 minutes or until golden.

Take out and cool. Add 1 c. raisins and/or Craisins™. Add M&M™ or chocolate chips if desired.

Corn Puffs ⚜

16 oz. bag of corn puffs	1 c. butter
1 c. sugar	¼ c. water

Boil sugar, butter, and water for 7-8 minutes. Heat corn puffs in microwave for 1 minute. Mix corn puffs and sugar mixture together in a big bowl. Spread puffs on wax paper to cool.

Hot Clam Dip ⚜

8 oz. pkg. cream cheese	½ c. sour cream
2 tbsp. mayonnaise	½ tsp. salt
1 small can chopped clams	½ tsp. Worcestershire sauce
¼ lb. sharp cheddar cheese	

Preheat oven to 350°. Combine cream cheese, sour cream, mayonnaise and Worcestershire sauce in a bowl. Blend until creamy with electric mixer. Fold in drained clams and salt. Spread into a baking dish and top with cheese. Bake at 350° for 20 minutes. Serve with an assortment of crackers.

Shrimp and Cream Cheese Appetizer ⚜

8 oz. cream cheese	1 lb. shrimp	8 oz. cocktail sauce	course ground black pepper (to taste)
1 tsp. Worcestershire sauce	salt (to taste)	½ c. fresh green onions	

Place cream cheese in dish. Combine all other ingredients. Pour over cream cheese, serve with any cracker or heavy chips.

Weights and Measures

A pinch = 1/8 teaspoon or less

3 teaspoons = 1 tablespoon

4 tablespoons = 1/4 cup

5 1/3 tablespoons = 1/3 cup

8 tablespoons = 1/2 cup

10 2/3 tablespoons = 2/3 cup

12 tablespoons = 3/4 cup

16 tablespoons = 1 cup

1 ounce = 28.35 grams

1 pound = 435.59 grams

1 gram = 0.0335 ounces

1 kilogram = 2.2 pounds

1 tablespoon = 1/2 fluid ounce

1 cup = 8 fluid ounces

1 cup = 1/2 pint

2 cups = 1 pint

4 cups = 1 quart

2 pints = 1 quart

4 quarts = 1 gallon

8 quarts = 1 peck

2 gallons = 1 peck

4 pecks = 1 bushel

1 tablespoon = 14.79 milliliters

1 cup = 236.6 milliliters

1 quart = 946.4 milliliters

1 liter = 1.06 quarts

❧ Notes ❧

Date of Gathering: _____

Guest List: _____

_____

Date of Gathering: _____

Guest List: _____

_____

Date of Gathering: _____

Guest List: _____

_____

Date of Gathering: _____

Guest List: _____

_____

Date of Gathering: _____

Guest List: _____

_____

❖ Comments ❖

_____

_____

_____

_____

_____

_____

_____

_____

_____

_____

_____

_____

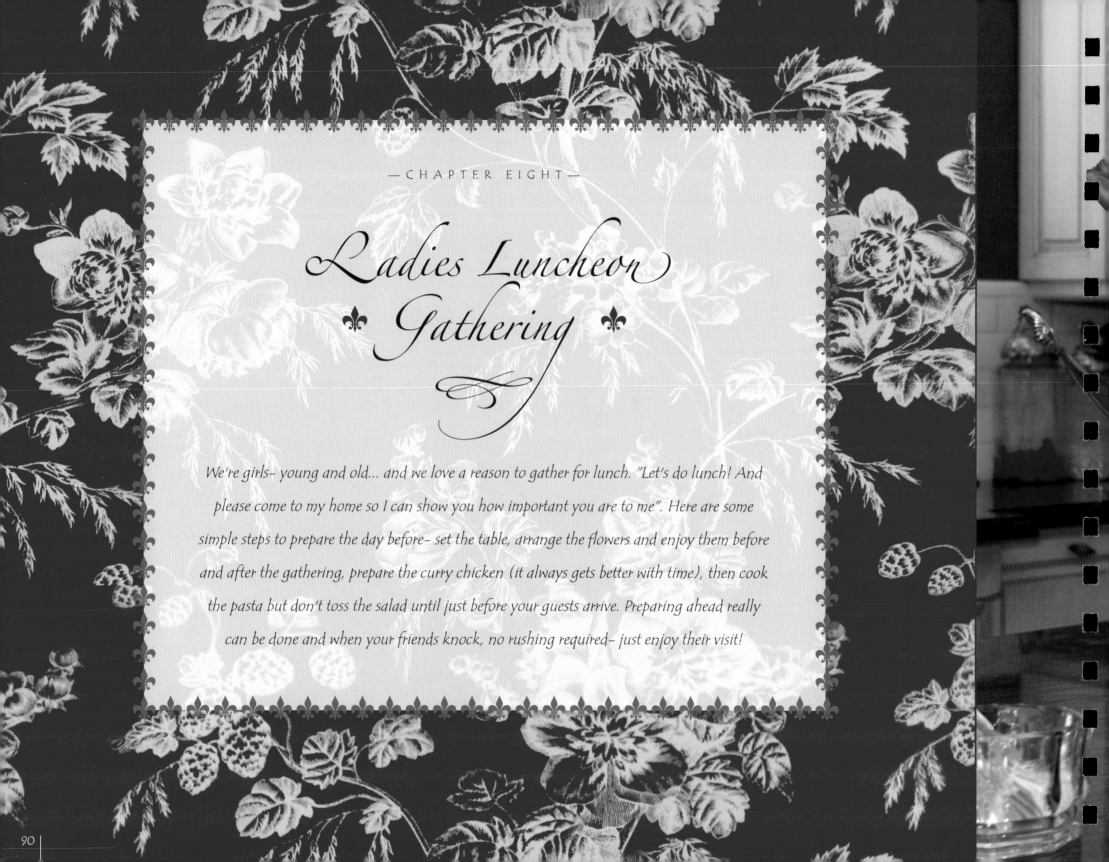

Ladies Luncheon
⚜ Gathering ⚜

We're girls– young and old... and we love a reason to gather for lunch. "Let's do lunch! And

please come to my home so I can show you how important you are to me". Here are some

simple steps to prepare the day before– set the table, arrange the flowers and enjoy them before

and after the gathering, prepare the curry chicken (it always gets better with time), then cook

the pasta but don't toss the salad until just before your guests arrive. Preparing ahead really

can be done and when your friends knock, no rushing required– just enjoy their visit!

Chicken and Apple Salad ⚜

2 lbs. chicken tenders

2 tart apples, cored & cubed

1 (8 oz.) round of Gouda cheese

1 (8 oz.) package bow tie pasta, cooked

½ c. celery, diced

1 c. pineapple tidbits

1 c. seedless grapes, halved

⅔ c. sliced almonds

Honey-Lime dressing:

1 c. mayonnaise

¼ c. sour cream

3 tbsp. lime juice

3 tbsp. honey

1 tbsp. poppy seeds

Combine all ingredients and stir well. Chill In large bowl combine bow tie pasta, apples, celery, grapes, almonds, pineapple tidbits and Gouda cheese. Toss with Honey-Lime dressing.

(Note: For best results add dressing just before serving)

Curry Chicken Wraps ⚜

4 lbs. chicken tenders	1/3 c. mustard
1½ c. mayonnaise	3/4 c. sugar
4 tbsp. curry powder	1 c. raisins
4 tsp. Worcestershire sauce	6 spinach wraps

Spray a large heavy pot with cooking spray, place frozen chicken tenders in pot, cover with lid, simmer for 10-12 minutes. Chicken will cook in its own juices and will be tender. In a bowl, add all other ingredients, whisk. Combine cooled chicken using a fork, until you have a 'tuna-like' consistency. Add raisins generously, fill wraps, fold the edges of the wrap and roll (like a burrito). Cut in half or in fourths using toothpicks to hold them together. (as pictured we used wheat and spinach wraps combined.)

Turkey Wraps ⚜

2 lbs. shaved deli turkey breast

8 oz. cream cheese

1 can cranberry sauce

½ small red onion, diced

sprouts and lettuce (optional)

6 spinach wraps

Spread a thin coat of cream cheese over at least half of the wrap, add a layer of cranberry sauce. Sprinkle the diced red onions. Place turkey in the center of the wrap, add salt and pepper. Top with sprouts and/or lettuce if desired. Fold the edges of the wrap and roll (like a burrito). Cut in half or in fourths, cover and chill until ready to serve.

Avocado Salad ⚜

3 c. grapefruit, cut into chunks

4 avocados, cut into chunks

Sweet poppy seed dressing:

    1½ c. oil

    2 c. white vinegar

    3 tsp. poppy seeds

    1 tsp. salt

    ¾ tsp. pepper

    1¼ c. sugar

    1 tsp. dry mustard

Combine all dressing ingredients together mixing well, and pour desired amount over the grapefruit and avocados. Toss gently and chill. Serve cold.

Icing:

3 c. powdered sugar

3 tbsp. milk

2 tsp. almond extract

When cake is hot right out of the oven take a roasting fork and poke deep holes in cake, quickly frost while still hot so the frosting will melt and seep into the cake.

Poppy Seed Bundt Cake ⚜

1 c. sugar	½ c. butter	2 c. cake flour
2 tsp. baking powder	½ tsp. salt	3 egg whites, beaten
1 tsp. almond extract	2 tbsp. poppy seeds (soaked in 1 c. milk for 2 hours)	

Preheat oven to 350°. Cream together sugar and butter. Sift cake flour, baking powder and salt together, add to creamed mixture. Add poppy seeds and milk. Fold in beaten egg whites and almond extract. Bake at 350° for 40 minutes.

Chocolate Bundt Cake ⚜

1 pkg. chocolate cake mix

1 (5 oz.) pkg. instant chocolate
        pudding mix

1 c. sour cream

½ c. oil

½ c. warm water

4 eggs

1 (6 oz.) pkg. chocolate chips

powdered sugar or hot fudge

Preheat oven to 350°. Mix first 6 ingredients together until blended. Fold in chocolate chips. Pour batter in greased bundt pan. Bake at 350° for 50 minutes. Sprinkle with powdered sugar, or drizzle hot fudge over the top (pg. 80)

Note: Great for cupcakes and frost with whip cream for a fun new treat!

Oatmeal Cake ⚜

½ c. butter

1¼ c. oatmeal

1½ c. boiling water

1 tsp. baking soda

1½ c. flour

1 c. brown sugar

1 c. sugar

1 tsp. cinnamon

2 eggs

1 tsp. salt

Preheat oven to 350°. In a bowl melt butter in microwave, combine oatmeal, add boiling water, and let sit for 20 minutes. Fold in remaining ingredients, mix well, and pour into a 9"x 13" or bundt cake pan. Bake at 350° for 30 minutes.

Topping:

¾ c. brown sugar   ⅓ c. butter

½ c. heavy whipping cream   1 c. pecans

1 c. coconut

Heat butter, sugar and heavy cream until the mixture begins to bubble on the sides, making sure that the butter is completely melted (do not bring to a boil). Fold in pecans and coconut, pour over hot cake. Place under the broiler for 2-3 minutes. (watch carefully, so that the coconut doesn't burn.)

Tulips with a Twist ⚜

Place limes in any larger glass container. Fill
with tulips, add water and enjoy a colorful
centerpiece.

Shopping List

For 10-12 people

2 tart apples	8 oz. cream cheese	dry mustard	chocolate cake mix
1 lime	16 oz. sour cream	1 c. raisins	chocolate chips
3 large grapefruits	heavy whipping cream	oatmeal	pineapple tidbits
1 c. seedless grapes	1 lb. butter	almond extract	cranberry sauce
celery	6 lbs. chicken tenders	2/3 c. sliced almonds	honey
4 avocados	2 lbs. deli turkey breast	1 c. pecans	Worcestershire sauce
1 red onion	12 oz. bow tie pasta	coconut	large mayonnaise jar
sprouts	hot fudge topping	white or yellow cake mix	12 spinach wraps
lettuce	poppy seeds	5 oz. vanilla instant pudding	white wine vinegar
8 oz. Gouda cheese	curry powder	5 oz chocolate instant pudding	yellow mustard

---

Staples:

sugar	egg	cinnamon
salt	vegetable oil	baking soda
pepper	flour	baking powder
milk	brown sugar	powdered sugar

❖ Notes ❖

Date of Gathering: _____

Guest List: _____

_____

Date of Gathering: _____

Guest List: _____

_____

Date of Gathering: _____

Guest List: _____

_____

Date of Gathering: _____

Guest List: _____

_____

Date of Gathering: _____

Guest List: _____

_____

❧ Comments ❧

_____
_____
_____
_____
_____
_____
_____
_____
_____
_____
_____
_____
_____

CHAPTER NINE

Going Home for Dinner

Preparing a meal to include everyone's favorite things combines years of familiar tastes

and smells and makes for a wonderful gathering in which to return home. Even after

leaving the nest our memory never dulls of the inviting aroma of fresh baked rolls or

the anticipation of indulging in the best mashed potatoes on the planet. The meal

on your table represents more than the longing we have for our favorite dishes; it

is reminiscent of memories made with loved ones while gathered around the table.

Pear Walnut Salad ⚜

2 large heads hearts of Romaine lettuce

1 lb. bacon, cut in ½ inch pieces and cooked

3 pears, cut into chunks with or without skin

12 oz. crumbled Gorgonzola cheese

1½ c. broken walnuts

Red Wine Dressing

Red Wine Dressing:

1½ c. red wine vinegar

1 c. sugar

¾ c. oil

1 medium red onion

½ tsp. salt

½ tsp. pepper

1½ tsp. dry mustard

2 tbsp. poppy seeds

Cut red onion into 1 inch cubes. Put all ingredients in a blender and Purée. Rinse hearts of Romaine lettuce, break into bite size pieces. Combine cooked bacon, pears, walnuts, and crumbled Gorgonzola cheese. Toss salad, add dressing, and serve.

Potato Rolls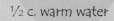

| ½ c. warm water | 4 tbsp. sugar | 4 packages active dry yeast | 2 c. cream | 1 tbsp. salt |
| 2 c. mashed potatoes | ½ c. butter | 8 c. all-purpose flour | 2 large eggs | |

Combine warm water with 2 tbsp. sugar and 4 packages active dry yeast in a small bowl. Stir and set aside. In a large bowl, mix the cream, mashed potatoes, melted butter, eggs, 2 tbsp. sugar, 1 tbsp. salt. Stir well and add the yeast mixture and 2 c. all-purpose flour. Work in another 6 c. flour, 2 c. at a time, until the dough is stiff enough to knead. Knead for 4 to 5 minutes on a lightly floured surface until the dough is smooth and elastic. Turn the dough into a lightly oiled bowl, cover, and let rise for an hour, until the dough doubles in size.

Preheat oven to 350°. Grease pie tins. Punch the dough down gently and push out all the air bubbles with your palm. Take pieces of dough to form 2 inch balls and set in a 9" pie tin, 1 inch apart, cover, and let rise for 30 to 40 minutes. Bake at 350° for 10 to 15 minutes, until browned. Brush the rolls with melted butter as soon as you remove them from the oven. Serve warm. Makes 3-4 doz. depending on size.

Chicken Angeline ⚜

6 whole chicken breasts

2 (8 oz.) jars marinated artichoke hearts,
        with juice

2 c. fresh mushrooms, sliced

1½ c. white cooking wine

¾ c. butter, sliced

1½ c. chicken broth

Chicken:

    5 eggs, beaten with ⅓ c. milk

    3 c. flour

    2 tsp. salt

    2 tbsp. granulated chicken bouillon

    1 tsp. pepper

    2 c. vegetable oil (for frying)

Preheat oven to 325°. Slice chicken breasts in half, cut each half diagonally in thirds, creating a thin flat piece of chicken. Pound with meat tenderizer until thin. In a bowl wisk milk and eggs together. Combine flour, chicken bouillon and pepper in a separate bowl, mix well. Dip chicken in egg mixture. Coat chicken in flower, covering completely. Heat oil in heavy skillet, fry chicken until golden, turning twice. Line a 9" x 13" pan with layered chicken pieces, spread mushrooms and artichokes (with marinade) on top. Pour chicken broth and white wine over chicken, helping create a clear gravy. Sprinkle 2 tbsp. granulated chicken bouillon over mixture. Using cold butter slices, spread evenly over top of Chicken Angeline. Cover with foil, bake 1 hour at 325°. Can be made a day in advance, just wait to pour the liquid over it until you are ready to bake. (If more gravy is desired, add more chicken broth after completely baked.) Serve chicken pieces on top of mashed potatoes topped with clear gravy.

Carrots and Green Beans ⚜

1 lb. fresh green beans

⅓ c. butter

1 lb. baby carrots

3 tsp. lemon pepper

Bring 4 c. of water to a boil, Add green beans and baby carrots boiling for 2½ to 3 minutes, drain and place in serving bowl. Slice butter and toss with lemon pepper. Serve.

Golden Mashed Potatoes ⚜

10 lbs. potatoes   1½ tsp. salt

¾ c. butter   1 tsp. pepper

½-1 c. cream or milk

Peel and cut potatoes in half. Cook for 20 min. or until soft. Mash, add butter, milk (as much as needed for consistency) ,salt and pepper to taste. Set aside 2 c. for potato rolls (pg. 105).

Fresh Strawberries with Sour Cream and Brown Sugar ⚜

Simply wash fresh strawberries, dip in sour cream, roll in brown sugar, and serve. This is a simple yet rich and tasty summer treat.

Limeade Pie

Crust:
  2 pkg. graham crackers
  ½ c. butter
  ¼ c. sugar

Preheat oven to 375°. Crush graham crackers until fine. Combine cracker crumbs and sugar with melted butter, press into 9" pie tin. Bake 10-12 minutes at 375°. Remove from oven and cool.

8 oz. container Cool Whip
14 oz. can sweetened condensed milk
6 oz. can frozen limeade concentrate
Juice of 1 lemon
9 inch graham cracker crust, baked

Fold together Cool Whip, condensed milk, limeade, and lemon juice. Pour into cooled pie crust and freeze.

Azalea Centerpiece ⚜

At anytime of the year Azaleas are available at your local grocery store. They bloom beautifully for three to four weeks if they are watered every five days. There are four 6 inch pots in this large container. They are fabulous as a centerpiece and are sure to brighten up any gathering.

Shopping List

For 10-12 people

1 lemon	1 lb. baby carrots	2 c. chicken broth	14 oz. sweet/condensed milk
3 pears	1 lb. bacon	1½ walnuts	granulated chicken bullion
2 lbs. strawberries	6 whole chicken breasts	white cooking wine	2 pkg. graham crackers
2 heads hearts of Romaine	16 oz. marinated artichoke hearts	red wine vinegar	6 oz. frozen limeade concentrate
1 red onion	12 oz. Gorgonzola cheese	active dry yeast	brown sugar
10 lbs. potatoes	heavy whipping cream	dry mustard	
16 oz. mushrooms	8 oz. sour cream	poppy seeds	
1 lb. fresh green beans	8 oz. cool Whip	lemon pepper	

Staples:

flour	pepper	eggs
sugar	olive oil	butter
salt	vegetable oil	milk

Notes

Date of Gathering: _____

Guest List: _____

_____

Date of Gathering: _____

Guest List: _____

_____

Date of Gathering: _____

Guest List: _____

_____

Date of Gathering: _____

Guest List: _____

_____

Date of Gathering: _____

Guest List: _____

_____

Comments

—CHAPTER TEN—

❧ Cookie Friendz ❧

For those of us that want to begin entertaining with a simple gathering, here is a magical idea. In trying to establish a traditional gathering that can be easily managed and enjoyed, this Cookie Friendz has brought people together for years. Everyone has a favorite cookie that they love to share. Guests are invited to bring four-six dozen of their favorite cookies (depending on number of attendees). The hostess will furnish lovely trays or celebration boxes that each guest will fill with a wonderful assortment of everyone's favorites. These recipes can be compiled before hand and then presented to each guest. What a great way to get to know new friends and neighbors.

Peanut Butter Cookies ⚜

1 c. butter, softened

1 c. creamy peanut butter

1 c. sugar

1 c. brown sugar

2 eggs

1 tsp. vanilla

½ tsp. salt

2 tsp. baking soda

2¾ c. flour

Preheat oven to 350°. Cream butter, peanut butter and sugars together, add eggs and vanilla, mix well. Stir in flour, soda, and salt, until well blended. Mold into balls and roll in sugar. Bake on ungreased cookie sheet for 10 minutes, remove from oven and place chocolate kiss in center of each cookie. Let cool.

Ryan's Cookies

2 c. brown sugar

2 c. sugar

2 c. butter

4 eggs

1 tbsp. vanilla

4 c. flour

1 tsp. salt

2 tsp. baking powder

2 tsp. baking soda

5 c. oatmeal

1 c. chocolate chips (optional)

1 c. mini M&Ms™ (optional)

Preheat oven to 400°. Cream together sugars, butter, eggs and vanilla. Mix separately, flour, salt, baking powder and baking soda. Blend with cream mixture, fold in oatmeal adding chocolate chips and mini M&Ms™. Bake at 400° for 5-6 minutes. Makes over five dozen.

Pecan Balls ⚜

½ c. butter   ½ c. and 2 tbsp. shortening

1 c. powdered sugar   2 tsp. vanilla

2½ c. cake flour   1 c. pecans

2 eggs

Preheat oven to 325°. Cream butter and shortening. Add eggs, sugar and vanilla, cream together thoroughly. Mix in flour, fold in pecans and roll dough into balls, place on ungreased cookie sheet. Bake at 325° for 15 minutes.

Frosting:

½ c. butter   3 tbsp. cream or milk

2 c. powdered sugar   1 tsp. vanilla

Cream together ingredients and spread over warm cookies, sprinkle with pecans.

Chex Mix Muddy Buddies

½ c. peanut butter

¼ c. butter

1 tsp. vanilla

8 oz. (1 c.) semisweet chocolate chips

2 c. powdered sugar

9 c. Chex™ cereal (rice, corn, or wheat)

Melt chocolate chips, peanut butter and butter in microwave for 1 minute. Stir. Microwave 30 seconds longer or until the mixture becomes smooth and creamy (be careful not to overcook). Fold in vanilla. Pour over cereal in large bowl, stir until evenly coated. Pour into a large plastic food-storage bag; add powdered sugar. Seal bag; shake until well coated.

Carmel Delights

2½ c. flour

2½ c. oatmeal

2½ c. brown sugar

½ tsp. salt

¾ tsp. baking soda

2½ c. butter, melted

1 (14 oz.) bag of cubed caramels

½ c. cream or milk

2 c. chocolate chips

nuts and coconut optional

Preheat oven to 350°. Mix all dry ingredients together, add melted butter. Line a 9" x 13" pan with half of the mixture and reserve the rest. Bake for 10-15 minutes at 350°. Remove and sprinkle chocolate chips over all.

In a separate bowl melt caramel and cream. Pour caramel over chocolate chips. Crumble the second half of the oatmeal mixture over the top of everything. Then top with as many nuts and as much coconut as desired. Bake for another 15 minutes. Cool, cut and serve.

English Toffee Bars

½ c. white sugar

¼ tsp. salt

1 (6 oz.) pkg.
chocolate chips

1 tsp. vanilla

1 c. butter

½ c. brown sugar

1 egg yolk

2 c. flour

½ c. walnuts

Preheat oven to 350°. Cream together vanilla, butter and egg yolk. Fold in sugars, salt and flour mixing thoroughly. Flatten cookie dough with fingers on greased cookie sheet. Bake 15 minutes at 350° or until golden. Remove from oven and while it is still hot, sprinkle chocolate chips on top of hot cookie, let melt for 2-3 minutes. Spread melted chocolate chips with spatula over entire cookie. Top with chopped nuts. Cut when still warm. These freeze very well.

Orange Ginger Cookies ⚜

1½ c. vegetable shortening

2 c. dark brown sugar (packed)

1 c. molasses

2 eggs

5 tbsp. finely grated orange rind

1½ tbsp. ground ginger

2 tsp. ground cinnamon

4 tsp. baking soda

5 c. flour

Orange Sugar Coating:

4 tbsp. finely grated orange rind

1 c. sugar

1 tsp. nutmeg

Preheat oven to 350°. Cream shortening, sugar, and ginger until soft and fluffy. Beat in molasses, add eggs one at a time mixing well after each addition. Fold in orange rind. Separately sift together flour, cinnamon and baking soda. Stir into creamed mixture, blend thoroughly. In a small bowl, combine orange rind, sugar and nutmeg. Roll balls of dough in sugar mixture. Place coated cookies on ungreased cookie sheet 3 inches apart. Bake for 10-12 minutes. Cool on cookie sheet for 5 minutes then move to cooling rack.

2¼ c. flour

½ tsp. salt

1 c. shortening

1 c. sugar

3 oz. cream cheese, softened

2 eggs

4 tsp. orange juice

3 tsp. grated orange rind

6 oz. chocolate chips

Preheat oven to 350°. Cream together shortening, sugar, cream cheese, eggs and orange juice. Combine flour and salt, mix thoroughly. Add chocolate chips and grated orange rind, mix completely. Bake on greased cookie sheet for 12 minutes at 350°.

Frosting:

2 c. powdered sugar

3 oz. cream cheese

1 tsp. orange juice

1 tbsp. orange rind

Mix all ingredients together and beat well. Frost cookies.

Rice Chex Treats

½ c. butter

1 lb. marshmallows

6 c. Rice Chex™ cereal

1 c. M&Ms™ or mixed nuts if desired

In a heavy pot, melt butter, fold in marshmallows, coating completely with warm butter. Cover pot and turn off heat. Wait a few minutes making sure marshmallows are melted. Stir in rice chex add M&Ms™, Spread on a cookie sheet.

Snickerdoodles

½ c. butter

1½ c. flour

1 c. sugar

1 egg

½ tsp. vanilla

¼ tsp. baking soda

¼ tsp. cream of tartar

2 tbsp. sugar

1 tsp. cinnamon

Preheat oven to 375° Cream butter for 30 seconds. Fold in sugar, egg, and vanilla Beat well. Add half of the flour, baking soda and cream of tartar. Beat until thoroughly combined. Fold in remaining flour mixing thoroughly. Cover and chill 1 hour. Combine sugar and cinnamon Shape dough into balls and roll balls in cinnamon, sugar mixture. Bake at 375 for 10-11 minutes.

Sugar Cookies ⚜

4 c. unsifted flour

1½ tsp. baking powder

1½ tsp. baking soda

½ tsp. salt

3 eggs, well beaten

1 c. buttermilk

1½ c. sugar

1 c. shortening

1 tsp. vanilla

Preheat oven to 350°. Sift dry ingredients together. Add eggs, buttermilk, shortening and vanilla. Mix Thoroughly. Cover and chill for 5 hours or overnight. Roll out ½ inch thick on floured surface. Cut into desired shapes. Bake at 350° for 8-10 minutes. Do not allow cookies to get brown. Frost as desired when cool.

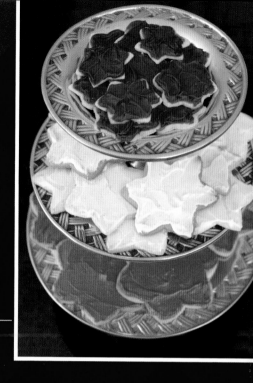

Frosting:

1 c. butter

1 tsp. almond or vanilla extract

3 c. powdered sugar

¼ c. milk (add a little at a time until you achieve desired consistency)

Cream together all ingredients adding milk slowly. Begin frosting the white stars and then separate leftover frosting into two bowls and add red food coloring to one and blue to the other. Frost cookies after they have cooled completely.

Chocolate Cookies

2 c. flour	2 c. sugar
2 eggs	1¼ c. butter
2 tsp. vanilla	¾ c. cocoa powder
½ tsp. salt	1 tsp. baking soda

Preheat oven to 350°. Beat butter, sugar, and eggs on medium speed for 2 minutes. Fold in vanilla. Sift flour, cocoa, salt and soda. Combine with creamed mixture. Chill dough 1 hour. Make into balls and roll in sugar. Bake at 350° for 8 minutes.

Chocolate Coconut Cookies

2¼ c. all-purpose flour	1 tsp. baking soda	¼ tsp. salt
1 c. butter, softened	¾ c. granulated sugar	¾ c. packed brown sugar
1 tsp. vanilla extract	2 large eggs	1½ c. angel flake sweetened coconut
1½ c. mini chocolate chips		

Preheat oven to 350°. Combine flour, baking soda, and salt in a small bowl. Cream butter, sugars, and vanilla extract in large mixing bowl. Add eggs one at a time, beating well after each egg. Gradually beat in flour mixture. Stir in chocolate and coconut and form into 1 inch round balls. Place on well-greased baking tray and bake at 350° for 8-10 minutes. Cool on baking sheets for 2 minutes and remove.

Cowboy Cookies ⚜

1 c. butter

1 c. white sugar

1 c. brown sugar

2 eggs

2 tsp. vanilla

2 c. flour

½ tsp. baking powder

1 tsp. baking soda

¼ tsp. salt

2 c. oatmeal

2 c. corn flakes, partially crushed

1 c. shredded coconut

1-2 c. chocolate chips and/or
    butterscotch chips (optional)

Preheat oven to 350°. Cream together thoroughly butter, sugars, eggs and vanilla Set aside. Sift together flour, soda, baking powder and salt, fold into butter mixture. Stir in oatmeal, crushed corn flakes, coconut and chocolate chips. Drop large spoonfuls on a greased cookie sheet, and bake at 350° for 8-10 minutes, or just until the cookies are barely light brown. It is better to take them out too early than too late.

Rice Krispy Treats ⚜

½ c. butter

1 lb. marshmallows

6 c. Rice Krispies™

melted chocolate chips (optional)

In a heavy pot, heat butter until bubbling fold in marshmallows and stir for 30 seconds. Cover with lid and turn off heat. Wait 5 minutes then stir in Rice Krispies™. Spread in a greased 9" x 13" pan or cookie sheet and drizzle with melted chocolate chips. Cool, cut into squares, and serve.

Peanut Butter Fingers ⚜

1 c. shortening
1 c. brown sugar
3 c. flour
1 c. peanut butter
½ tsp baking soda
¾ tsp. salt

2 eggs
½ c. water
1 c. sugar
3 c. oatmeal
1 tsp. vanilla

Preheat oven to 325°. Cream shortening, peanut butter, sugars, eggs, and water. Add dry ingredients, press into a 9"x13" pan. Bake at 325° for 12-15 min. Cool. Spread frosting over the top, cut, and serve.

Frosting:

½ c. butter, softened
3 c. powdered sugar
2 tbsp. milk
1 tsp. vanilla
¾ -1 c. cocoa

Whip ingredients with electric mixer until light and fluffy. Add more milk for desired consistency.

English Toffee ⚜

1 c. chopped pecans
1 c. sugar
1 c. butter
3 tbsp. water
1 tsp. vanilla
1½ c. chocolate chips

Lightly spray 9"x 9" pan with cooking spray. Sprinkle chopped pecans on the bottom of pan, set aside. Combine butter, sugar and water in sauce pan, bring to a boil over medium heat, stirring to hard ball stage. Spread over pecans. Quickly spread chocolate chips evenly over hot toffee. Let melt. Spread like frosting over toffee.

Shortbread Cookies ⚜

1 c. butter

¾ c. sugar

2 c. flour

Preheat oven to 325°. Cream butter and gradually add in sugar. By hand, handling as little as possible, fold in flour. If dough is crumbly add 1-2 tbsp. of softened butter. Chill in fridge for 30 minutes. Using rolling pin, spread to desired thickness (about ¼ inch thick). Cut into desired shape. Bake at 325° for 15-18 minutes, or until golden brown.

Frosting:

½ c. butter

3 c. powdered sugar

1½ tsp. vanilla

3 tbsp. milk or cream

Blend all of the ingredients until creamy and frost.

Mini-Bundt Chocolate Brownie ⚜

½ c. butter	½ tsp. salt	Preheat oven to 325°. Cream butter, sugar,	mini-bundt/muffin trays, bake for 20-25
1 c. sugar	2 eggs	vanilla and cocoa powder; add eggs and beat	minutes at 325°. Remove immediately from
1 tsp. vanilla	4 tbsp. cocoa	lightly. Mix dry ingredients together and add	trays, cover with plastic wrap to retain mois-
½ tsp. baking soda	¾ c. flour	to creamy mixture. Pour batter into greased	ture. (Do not over bake.)

Pumpkin Chocolate Chip Cookies ⚜

1 spice cake mix

1 pkg. chocolate chips

1 egg

1 (15oz.) can pumpkin

1 tsp. pumpkin spice

Preheat oven 350°. Mix together well. Grease cookie sheet. Drop by teaspoonfuls on sheet. Bake cookies 10-12 minutes. Makes 2½ dozen. Great low fat cookies!

Rolo Cookies ⚜

1 c. butter, softened

¾ c. brown sugar

¾ c. white sugar

1 pkg. Rolos™ candies

1 tsp. vanilla

1 tbsp. water

2 c. flour

1 tsp. baking soda

½ tsp. salt

2 eggs

Preheat oven to 350°. Cream butter and sugars. Add eggs, vanilla and water. Beat until light and fluffy. Mix flour with baking soda and salt and add to creamed mixture. Shape cookies into small balls. Press Rolo™ into center of ball and cover. Bake on a ungreased cookie sheet at 350° for 8-10 minutes.

Seven-Layer Bars ⚜

½ c. butter

1½ c. graham cracker-crumbs

1 (6 oz.) package butterscotch chips

1 (6 oz.) package chocolate chips

1 (7 oz.) package shredded coconut

1 c. chopped nuts

1 (14 oz). can sweetened condensed milk

Preheat oven to 350°. Pour melted butter in a 9"x 13" pan. Sprinkle graham cracker crumbs over butter and layer butterscotch and chocolate chips over crumbs. Sprinkle coconut and nuts over chips. Pour milk over this mixture and bake at 350° for 25 minutes. Cut into squares.

Almond Cake ⚜

1 c. sugar
1 c. flour
2 beaten eggs
½ c. butter, melted
1 tsp. almond extract

Preheat oven to 350°. Combine
all of the ingredients together and
hand mix with a fork as little as possible. Cover with slivered almonds.
Bake at 350° for 25-30 minutes.
Makes 1 pie tin or round cake pan.

*Option: You may make ahead of time
and freeze. They thaw beautifully.*

No Bake Cookies ⚜

2 c. sugar

½ c. milk

½ c. butter

3 c. instant oatmeal

1 tsp. vanilla

5 tbsp. cocoa

Bring to a boil sugar, milk, and butter. In a bowl combine oatmeal, vanilla, and coco. Pour hot mixture in bowl and stir. Drop by teaspoonful onto a cookie sheet. Cookies will harden as they cool.

Option: Add 1 cup of nuts, coconut or raisins as desired.

Notes

Date of Gathering: _____

Guest List: _____

_____

Date of Gathering: _____

Guest List: _____

_____

Date of Gathering: _____

Guest List: _____

_____

Date of Gathering: _____

Guest List: _____

_____

Date of Gathering: _____

Guest List: _____

_____

Comments

CHAPTER ELEVEN

An Afternoon
with Friends

Gathering in an informal setting can create an atmosphere where friendship and conversation blossom with ease. Preparing a menu that seems familiar is essential to nourishing both heart and soul. Enjoying healthy food, combined with meaningful conversation can enhance any gathering and strengthen the bonds that connect us as friends. A casual afternoon spent in the company of good friends is one of life's most welcome pleasures.

Mexican Chicken Crescent Squares ⚜

2 c. chicken, shredded

¼ c. red peppers, diced

6 oz. cream cheese, softened

⅛ tsp. cumin

½ c. butter, softened

2-8 oz. cans refrigerated crescent rolls

1 can green chilies, diced

1 c. dry seasoned stuffing, crushed

1 tbsp. green onions, chopped

⅛ tsp. chili powder

Mix together cream cheese, green chilies, green onions, chili powder, red peppers and cumin. Add chicken and combine.

Preheat oven to 350°. Separate crescent rolls to form 8 rectangles, pressing seams together. Place ½ c. of chicken mixture in the middle of each rectangle and roll up ends. Seal edges. Dip each square in melted butter and then roll in crushed stuffing. Place on baking sheet and bake for 20 minutes at 350°. Garnish with Southwestern Salsa Medley and fresh avocado.

Southwest Salsa Medley ⚜

2 tbsp. red wine vinegar

1½ tsp. vegetable oil

1-2 tsp. hot sauce

1 clove garlic, minced

2 firm, ripe avocados

6 roma tomatoes, chopped

2 tsp. fresh lime juice

1 can black beans

1 can corn

1 can black-eyed peas

²/₃ c. cilantro

²/₃ c. green onion

salt and pepper to taste

1 can green chilies, diced

Mix vinegar, oil, hot sauce and garlic in bowl. Cut avocado's into ½ inch cubes and add to vinegar mixture. Drain and rinse the peas, beans and corn and add to the mixture. Then add cilantro, green onions and tomatoes. Add salt and pepper to taste. Serve over chicken crescents or with tortilla chips.

Barley and Mushroom Pilaf ⚜

2 onions, chopped

½ lb. fresh mushrooms, sliced

¼ c. butter, divided

1¼ c. pearl barley

½ c. red peppers, diced

½ c. almonds, sliced (optional)

1 qt. chicken broth (or 6 cubes chicken bouillon + 4 c. water)

salt and pepper to taste

*Option: substitute ¾ c. wild rice for ¾ c. barley for a twist.

Preheat oven to 350°. Melt 3 tbsp. butter, sauté onions and mushrooms. Remove and place in a large casserole dish. Melt remaining butter and brown barley until golden, stirring constantly. Add to mushrooms and onions. Pour 1½ c. of chicken broth over all, cover and bake at 350° for 30 minutes. Remove lid, season with salt and pepper and add another 1½ c. of broth. Cover and bake an additional 30 minutes. Uncover and cook an additional 10 to 15 minutes, adding more broth if dry. Garnish with diced red peppers for color and serve.

Green Bean Salad ⚜

1 lb. fresh green beans
1 c. shredded carrots
1 c. slivered almonds
1 tbsp. water
3 tbsp. sugar

Wash and clip off the ends of the green beans. Steam until fork tender, approximately 3-4 minutes. Steam the shredded carrots for 1-2 minutes. Add carrots to green beans and toss in a little butter. To make the sugared almonds put sugar, water, and almonds in a saucepan and mix. Cook for about 4-5 minutes or until sugar lightly boils. Then pour onto a cooking sheet to let cool completely. Break up pieces and toss with hot vegetables and serve.

Pumpkin Surprise ⚜

2 c. canned pumpkin

½ tsp. salt

1 can sweetened condensed milk

1 c. sugar

3 eggs, beaten

2 tsp. Pumpkin Pie spice

1 white or yellow cake mix

¾ c. of cold butter

Preheat oven to 350°. Combine the first 6 ingredients and pour into a greased 9x13 pan. Sprinkle the dry cake mix over the top. Slice cold butter and cover the dry cake evenly with butter squares.

Whipped Cream:

1 pint whipping cream   ½ c. sugar

1 tsp. vanilla   ½ tsp. nutmeg

Whip cream until stiff, fold in sugar and vanilla, top with nutmeg.

Bake at 350° for 45 minutes. Serve warm. Top with vanilla ice cream or whipped cream. Sprinkle with nutmeg.

Sunflower Topiary ⚜

Use any type of clay pot for this centerpiece. Pick a hand full of sunflowers keeping stems long, wrap with floral tape and cover with ribbon. Brace in pot using styrofoam and cover with moss. Add any seasonal flower at the base. Makes for a great centerpiece.

Shopping List

For 10-12 people

1 lime	1 c. shredded carrots	1 can black-eyed peas	pumpkin pie spice
2 firm ripe avocados	½ lb. fresh mushrooms	1 can black beans	Nutmeg
6 roma tomatoes	6 chicken breast	1 can corn	2 c. canned pumpkin
2 red bell pepper	6 oz. cream cheese	1 c. dry stuffing mix	1 can sweetened condensed
2 bunches green onions	1 pint heavy whipping cream	1½ c. pearl barley	milk
2 onions	cumin	4 c. chicken broth	1 white or yellow cake mix
1 clove garlic	16 oz. refrigerated crescent rolls	chili powder	red wine vinegar
1 bundle cilantro	2 (7 oz.) cans diced	almonds	hot sauce
1 lb. green beans	green chilies	slivered almonds	vegetable oil

Staples:

butter	pepper	eggs
salt	sugar	vanilla

Notes

Date of Gathering: _____

Guest List: _____

_____

Date of Gathering: _____

Guest List: _____

_____

Date of Gathering: _____

Guest List: _____

_____

Date of Gathering: _____

Guest List: _____

_____

Date of Gathering: _____

Guest List: _____

_____

Comments

—CHAPTER TWELVE—

Springtime Breakfast

After what seems to be a long winter and the gray pall over head transforms

into vibrant blue sky with wisps of white clouds… the gentle breeze of spring

is in the air. Celebrate nature's renewal and the fondness of friends with early

hour gatherings Bright colors, lighter meals, fresh flowers…

this menu offers something everyone is sure to love. A morning bathed in the

radiance of sunshine and cloaked with the cheer of friendship sets the tone for

a bright and beautiful day. Surround yourself with love; gather with friends.

Pesto, Tomato and Mozzarella ⚜

1 jar pesto sauce

4 vine ripened tomatoes

Triscuits™

1 lb. fresh mozzarella

Balsamic vinegar

Salt & pepper to taste

Begin with a Triscuit™ followed by a slice of fresh tomato, add a slice of mozzarella topped with a daub of pesto sauce. Finish with a drizzle of balsamic vinegar. Salt and pepper to taste.

Toasted Sesame Chicken Pasta ⚜

3 lbs. chicken tenders

16 oz. Radiatore pasta
(may substitute bow tie, penne, etc.)

2 bundles of asparagus

2 c. Candied Pecans

Sesame Ginger Dressing

Spray a heavy pot with cooking spray. Place frozen chicken tenders in pot, cover with lid. Cook on medium heat for 10-12 minutes. Prepare candied pecans, so they have time to cool. Drain and shred chicken into chunks with fork, cover and set aside. Cook Pasta. Rinse asparagus, clip ends, blanch in boiling water for two minutes, cut in 2 inch chunks and set aside. Prepare Sesame Ginger Dressing. Combine all ingredients in large bowl and toss. Serve warm or cool.

Candied Pecans:

½ c. butter melted   2 c. pecans

¾ c. brown sugar

Preheat oven to 375°. Combine melted butter and brown sugar stirring until sugar dissolves. Fold in pecans and spread on a 9"x13" pan and bake at 375° for 10 minutes. Let cool and break up into pieces. Set aside.

Sesame Ginger Dressing:

½ c. frozen orange juice concentrate

½ c. toasted sesame seed oil

½ c. rice wine vinegar

¼ c. olive oil

⅓ c. soy sauce

⅓ c. Worcestershire sauce

2 tbsp. lemon juice

2 cloves garlic, pressed

1 tsp. ginger

4 tbsp. toasted sesame seeds

In a small skillet toast the sesame seeds until golden or dark brown, it only takes about two minutes on medium heat. Set aside to cool. In a blender mix all other ingredients except the sesame seeds. Purée. Pour dressing in a container with lid, add toasted sesame seeds only stirring with a spoon. Shake well before serving.

Rolled Ham and Cream Cheese Sandwiches ⚜

1 recipe Bread Dough
2 lbs. thinly sliced ham

1 c. cream cheese
½ c. A1 Sauce™

½ c. butter, melted
1½ c. fresh Parmesan cheese

Bread Dough:
3 small potatoes,
   peeled and cubed
3 pkgs. dry yeast
4½ tsp. salt
3 c. water
3¾ c. milk
3 eggs
12–13½ c. flour
¾ c. sugar
¾ c. shortening

In a sauce pan, cook potatoes covered in water until tender (10-15 min.), drain and mash. Measure 1½ c. mashed potatoes and set aside. In a large bowl combine 6 c. flour and yeast. In saucepan heat milk, sugar, shortening and salt until warm, stirring constantly until shortening almost melts. Add to dry mixture, add egg and potato. Beat on low with mixer for ½ minute, scraping sides constantly. Beat on high for 3 min. By hand, add remaining flour to make a soft dough. Knead 6-8 min. Shape into a ball and place in a lightly greased bowl turning once to grease surface. Cover and let rise in a warm place until doubled in size (about an hour). Punch down, turn out on lightly floured surface. Let rise 10 minutes.

Preheat oven to 350°. After dough has risen, take big pieces of the dough and flatten them. Brush with melted butter and place 3 large thin ham slices on each. Spread cream cheese over ham and drizzle 1 tsp. A1 Sauce™ through the center of the ham. Wrap dough around ham, forming a roll and tighten the edges. Brush with butter and roll in fresh Parmesan cheese. Place on cookie sheet and let rise 1 hour. Bake at 350° until golden, approximately 20-30 minutes.

Blueberry Salad ⚜

24 oz. mixed-berry yogurt
24 oz. container of Cool Whip™
2-3 c. of blueberries (fresh or frozen)
1 c. sugar

Mix together gently. Chill in refrigerator for 2-3 hours. Add food coloring to liven up color as desired.

Chocolate Strawberry Trifle ⚜

2 quarts fresh strawberries, sliced

3-4 tbsp. sugar

1 angel food cake, cut into 1 inch cubes

1 c. heavy cream

1 tsp. vanilla extract

1 tbsp. sugar

5 oz. box chocolate pudding , make according to directions on package

Slice strawberries, coat with sugar. In a bowl whip the heavy cream until stiff, fold in vanilla and sugar. Layer in a trifle bowl, starting with a layer of angel food cake, followed by a layer of strawberries, chocolate pudding and whip cream. Continue layering, ending with strawberries. Cover with plastic wrap and chill well before serving. Garnish with whip cream and raspberries.

Party Pretzels ⚜

1 bag small pretzels

1 c. coconut

1 bag semi-sweet or white chocolate chips

Melt chocolate in the microwave. Dip pretzels in chocolate, roll in coconut. Let cool until chocolate is hard. Put in a cellophane bag and tie off with your favorite ribbon.

Hydrangea Centerpieces ⚜

Purchase any color hydrangea at your favorite garden shop. Place in a fun pot and use as your centerpiece or as a gift for your guests. Remember that hydrangeas must be watered everyday. The flowers will last 8-10 weeks if you take care of them. For every day they don't receive water, they loose a week of their flowering life.

❦ Shopping List ❦

For 10-12 people

1 lemon	8 oz. cream cheese	toasted sesame seed oil	2 lbs. thinly sliced deli ham
2 quarts fresh strawberries	fresh Parmesan cheese	2 c. pecans	3 lbs. chicken tenders
2 c. fresh blueberries	heavy cream	coconut (shredded for baking)	16 oz. radiatore pasta
2 bunches asparagus	24 oz. mixed-berry yogurt	16 oz. bag chocolate chips	orange juice concentrate
4 vine ripened tomatoes	A1 Sauce™	ginger	24 oz. Cool Whip™
3 small potatoes	1 jar pesto sauce	sesame seeds	5 oz. box chocolate pudding
garlic cloves	soy sauce	3 packages dry yeast	Worcestershire sauce
angel food cake	rice wine vinegar	Triscuits™	
fresh mozzarella	balsamic vinegar	pretzels	

Staples:

salt	butter	eggs
pepper	olive oil	vanilla
sugar	flour	shortening
brown sugar	milk	

Notes

Date of Gathering: _____

Guest List: _____

_____

Date of Gathering: _____

Guest List: _____

_____

Date of Gathering: _____

Guest List: _____

_____

Date of Gathering: _____

Guest List: _____

_____

Date of Gathering: _____

Guest List: _____

_____

Comments

_____

_____

_____

_____

_____

_____

_____

_____

_____

_____

_____

_____

_____

_____

CHAPTER THIRTEEN

No Bake Baby Shower

Here's a party that anyone can host- no baking is required! Some
planning is necessary, a pinch of creative thinking, and a few trips
to your favorite stores... but everything can be purchased right down
to the bacon bits and sprinkled cupcakes. If you are inclined, here
are a few recipes to satisfy your creative urges. They are quick and
easy to prepare leaving you plenty of time for associating with guests
and enjoying the moment.

Cobb Salad ⚜

2 heads iceberg lettuce, washed and torn into bite sized pieces

1 lb. bacon, crisply cooked and crumbled

12 oz. crumbled blue cheese

6 hard boiled eggs

1 large can olives, diced

4–5 large tomatoes, diced

4 c. cooked chicken or turkey, cubed

In a large bowl assemble lettuce, topped by arranged ingredients row by row.

Serve with your favorite dressing.

Chile Cheesecake ⚜

1 c. tortilla chips, crushed

2 chopped tomatoes

2 (8 oz.) pkg. cream cheese, softened

1 (7 oz.) can diced green chiles

1 fresh jalapeno pepper, cored, seeded, and diced

1/3 c. olives

3 tbsp. butter, melted

4 green onions, diced

2 eggs

4 oz. Colby cheese, shredded

4 oz. Monterrey Jack cheese, shredded

1/4 c. sour cream

Preheat oven to 325°. In medium bowl, combine tortilla chips and butter.

Press into bottom of 9" springform pan. Bake 15 minutes, remove from

Red Pepper Hummus ⚜

Prepare up to three days in advance and refrigerate in an airtight container.
Serve with vegetables.

1 red bell pepper

2½ tbsp. fresh lemon juice

1 tbsp. Tahini (sesame seed paste)

½ tsp. freshly ground black pepper

¼ tsp. salt

¼ tsp. ground cumin

1 (18 oz.) can chickpeas or garbanzo beans, rinsed and drained

1 garlic clove, quartered

oven, leaving oven on. In large bowl, blend cream cheese and eggs. Add green chiles, jalapeno, Colby and Monterrey Jack. Pour over crust and bake 30 minutes. Do not overcook. Remove from oven and cool in pan 5 minutes. Run knife around inside edge and remove sides from pan. Spread sour cream over top and garnish with tomatoes, green onions, and olives. Serve with tortilla chips.

Preheat broiler. Cut bell pepper in half, discard center seeds and place them skin side up on foil lined baking sheet and press flat. Broil for ten minutes or until blackened. Place in a zip-lock and set aside for ten minutes. Peel. Place bell pepper and remaining ingredients in a food processor; process until smooth.

Place the hummus in a nice dish and garnish with toasted pine nuts. This delicious dip can be served with an assortment of sides such as pita chips, crackers, tortilla chips. Here we have chosen to serve it with a variety of vegetables.

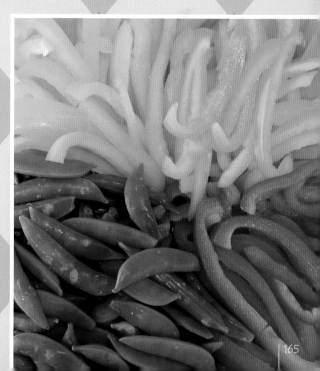

Black Cupcakes ⚜

4 oz. bittersweet chocolate, chopped

½ c. butter, room temperature

½ c. sugar

2 eggs

2 tbsp. ground almonds

1¼ c. flour

2 tbsp. cocoa powder

Melt the chocolate in a double boiler or in microwave, let stand to cool. Beat the butter and sugar together in a bowl until fluffy, then beat in the eggs, one at a time. Add the melted chocolate, and almonds. Sift the flour and cocoa into the mixture.

Preheat oven to 350°. Line the muffin pan with paper liners. Spoon the mixture into the muffin cups and bake at 350° for 18-20 minutes, or until a skewer inserted in the center comes out clean. Transfer to cooling rack.

Frosting:

3½ oz. bittersweet chocolate, chopped and melted

½ c. heavy cream

3 c. powdered sugar

Beat until smooth and creamy. Pipe frosting onto cooled cupcakes. Top with grated chocolate bar, and serve.

Cream Cakes ⚜

1 c. butter, softened

3 c. sugar

6 eggs

3 c. flour, sifted

1 c. heavy whipping cream

1½ tsp. almond extract

½ tsp. nutmeg

Preheat oven to 325°. Cream together butter and sugar in a mixing bowl until light and fluffy. Add the eggs and beat well. Add flour and whipping cream and mix well. Stir in the almond and nutmeg. Spoon into greased muffin trays of any shape, only halfway because it rises a lot. Bake at 325° for 40 minutes. Cool in trays for at least 20 minutes.

Lemon Pound Cupcakes ⚜

1¾ c. sugar   1 c. butter, softened

3 eggs   3 c. flour

½ tsp. salt   ½ tsp. baking soda

1 c. buttermilk   ⅓ c. fresh lemon juice

4 tbsp. finely grated lemon rind

Preheat oven to 325°. Grease and flour 10 inch bundt pan. In large bowl, cream 1 c. of the butter and sugar until fluffy. Beat in eggs, 1 at a time. Combine flour, baking soda, and salt. Add to butter mixture slowly, alternating with buttermilk, beating between each addition. Add 3 tbsp. of the lemon zest and ¼ c. of the lemon juice. Beat until well blended. Pour into cupcake liners. Bake at 325° for 30-35 minutes. Cool in pan, about 20 minutes.

Frosting:

3 c. powdered sugar   ½ c. butter, room temperature

½ tsp. vanilla   2½ tbsp. lemon juice

Blend butter, powdered sugar, vanilla, and lemon juice together in a mixing bowl. Add more sugar if needed for fluffy frosting. After frosting cooled cupcakes grate lemon rind over the tops of each cupcake or use any preferred sprinkle.

Carrot Cupcakes ⚜

2 c. sugar   4 eggs

1 c. cooking oil   2 c. flour

2 tsp. cinnamon   1 tsp. salt

2 tsp. vanilla   3 c. grated carrots

1½ c. raisins   nuts (optional)

Preheat oven to 350°. Mix sugar and eggs in a medium mixing bowl and then beat in the oil. Add the dry ingredients to mixture and blend well. Add vanilla, carrots, nuts, and raisins to mixture. Pour mixture into cupcake pans and bake for 20-25 minutes at 350°. Let cool and then frost.

Frosting:

1 oz. cream cheese, softened

½ c. butter

2 c. powdered sugar

lemon juice or milk as needed

Mix cream cheese, butter, and powdered sugar together. If frosting is too thick add milk or lemon juice until mixture is easily able to spread.

Candy and Soda ⚜

Allowing your guests to fill their own gift bags is a great idea! A large tub filled with ice and drinks helps get any party started.

Diaper Cake ⚜

This Diaper Cake makes for a great gift (and centerpiece) at a baby shower. Take about a dozen diapers of any size and wrap them with thick ribbon. Then take about 30 to 35 diapers and tape them together with clear tape and tie with thick ribbon. Make three or four levels of these diaper bundles getting wider with each level. Stack these diaper tiers and make it look like a four layered cake, using heavy tape to connect each layer. Top with a bow. It makes for a fun centerpiece and great gift for the mother-to-be.

Nacho Cups/Trays ⚜

Choose any cute, heavy card stock that matches your color scheme. Cut card stock into 4½"x 4½" squares and clip the corners first at a 45° angle, then slit at the opposing 45° angle. (See the pattern on the facing page). Paste or staple corners to form the trays/cups.

Nachos ⚜

16 oz. Velveeta™ cheese

6 green onions chopped

7 oz. can chopped green chilies

½ tsp. salt

2 tbsp. sugar

2 fresh diced tomatoes

½ minced fresh cilantro

4 fresh green chili peppers chopped (optional)

½ tsp. coarse black pepper

Cut Velveeta™ into small squares and heat in microwave 2-3 minutes or until smooth. Dice tomatoes, sprinkle with sugar and set aside. Chop and combine the remaining ingredients and fold into warm cheese sauce. Pour cheese sauce over tortilla chips, top with sugared tomatoes, and serve. (or use queso dip)

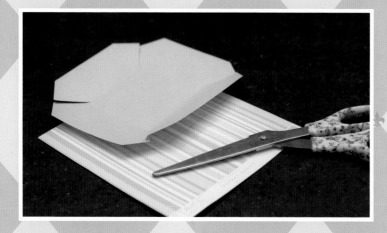

Step 1: Cut card stock into 4½" x 4½" squares and clip the corners first at a 45° angle, then slit at the opposing 45° angle.

Step 2: Paste or staple corners to form the trays/cups.

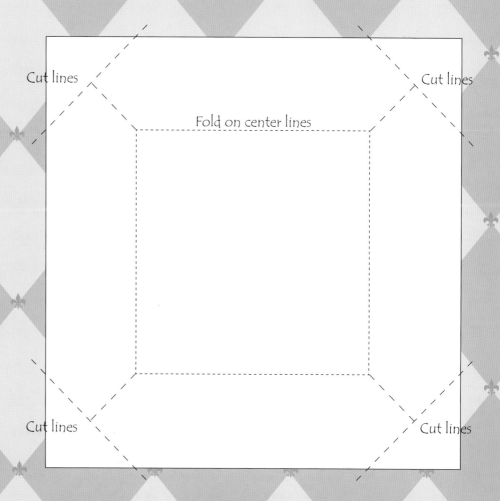

Cut lines

Cut lines

Fold on center lines

Cut lines

Cut lines

Strawberry Topiary Tree ⚜

Purchase a styrofoam topiary with one or two balls as well as a base from any craft store. Cover the base with plastic wrap and place in desired bowl or pot. Using toothpicks, place strawberries stem down into the styrofoam balls as pictured. Fill the base with approximately 2 c. of sour cream (depending on size of bowl) and cover with approximately 1½ c. brown sugar as shown to resemble "dirt". Tie with any coordinating ribbon and you have a great centerpiece that tastes delicious.

Shopping List

For 10-12 people

1 red bell pepper	4 green chillies	16 oz. sour cream	2 can black olives
2 quarts fresh strawberries	9 tomatoes	nutmeg	18 oz. chickpeas or
3 lemon	3 c. grated carrots	cumin	garbanzo beans
2 heads ice berg lettuce	Tahini™ (sesame seed paste)	almond extract	queso dip
1 lb. bacon	12 oz. blue cheese	ground almond	tortilla chips
2 large avocados	8 oz. Colby cheese	cocoa powder	candy assortments
1 fresh jalapeno pepper	8 oz. Monterrey jack cheese	8 oz. bittersweet chocolate	soda bottles
garlic clove	8 oz. cream cheese	2 lbs. powdered sugar	16 oz. Velveeta™ cheese
green onions	heavy whipping cream	4 c. turkey or chicken cooked	7 oz. can diced green chillies
cilantro	buttermilk	or cubed	rasins

Staples:			
	eggs	brown sugar	baking soda
	butter	sugar	vegetable oil
	salt	baking soda	cinnamon
	pepper	butter	
	flour	vanilla	

Notes

Date of Gathering: _____

Guest List: _____

_____

Date of Gathering: _____

Guest List: _____

_____

Date of Gathering: _____

Guest List: _____

_____

Date of Gathering: _____

Guest List: _____

_____

Date of Gathering: _____

Guest List: _____

_____

Comments

CHAPTER FOURTEEN

❧ Garden Brunch ❧

Inviting new neighbors for a casual morning meal is a nice way to become better acquainted. Welcome them to your table with this brunch… created around fresh tomatoes from the garden, combined with fresh fruit, breakfast potatoes, egg and cheese casserole, and fried tomato sandwiches. It can all be enjoyed in the late morning hours before the busy activities of life get in the way. Open your home; open your heart… and make new friends along the way.

John Wayne Casserole ⚜

1 (8 oz.) can Jalapeno (or green) chilies, drained and diced	1 tbsp. flour
1 lb. Cheddar cheese, grated	½ tsp. salt
1 lb. Monterrey Jack cheese, grated	½ tsp. pepper
4 eggs, separate whites and yolks	4 tomatoes, sliced
1 can evaporated milk	4–5 tbsp. white sugar

Breakfast Potatoes ⚜

3-4 lbs. baby red potatoes

½ c. butter

½-1 c. milk or cream

1 lb. spicy ground sausage

1½ tsp. salt

1 tsp. pepper

1 onion, minced (optional)

Clean and peel potatoes leaving ⅓ of the skins on. Boil in water until fork tender. Drain. Whip with electric mixer, adding butter and milk or cream (use just enough for desired consistency). Sauté sausage and onion. Drain grease and fold sausage into potatoes.

Preheat oven to 325°. Blending cheeses together, combine chilies and cheese and place in a well buttered 9"x 13" casserole dish. Beat egg whites at high speed to stiff peaks. Gently fold in egg yolks, milk, flour, salt and pepper, mixing thoroughly. Pour into casserole over grated cheeses. Bake at 325° for 30 minutes. Remove and carefully place sliced tomatoes over the top of the casserole. Sprinkle tomatoes with sugar. Top with fresh coarse ground pepper. Return to oven and bake for additional 15 minutes.

Summer Fruit Salad ⚜

Combine the following in a trifle bowl:

3 c. fresh pineapple   3 c. fresh cantaloupe   3 c. fresh honeydew

Dip:

1 (8 oz.) pkg. cream cheese   1 tbsp. lemon juice

1 c. marshmallow whip

Blend together, chill, and serve.

Fried Tomato Sandwiches ⚜

¼ c. butter

3-4 ripe tomatoes, sliced

5 oz. cream cheese, softened

⅓ to ½ c. sugar

salt and pepper

1 baguette cut in ¼ inch slices (20 slices)

Melt butter in frying pan. Place sliced tomatoes in pan and sprinkle with ½ of the sugar, salt and pepper. Sauté for 4-5 minutes, flip and sprinkle with remaining sugar, salt and pepper. Sauté for an additional 4-5 minutes. If tomatoes seem runny, continue to sauté on low heat until sauce thickens. Place baguette slices on a cookie sheet and broil until golden. Spread with softened cream cheese and return to oven until cream cheese bubbles. Spread fried tomatoes over open faced toasted baguette.

Hydrangea Decoration ⚜

Buy artificial hydrangea plants and any additional contrasting flower for color. (we used small red open roses.) at your local craft store. Cut off sections and simply tie a bow using your favorite ribbon. A great way to liven up any place setting!

Shopping List

For 10-12 people

4 lbs. baby red potatoes	8 oz. cream cheese	chilies	marshmallow whip
8 large tomatoes	5 oz. cream cheese	1 baguette	lemon juice
1 onion	1 lb. Monterrey Jack cheese	fresh pineapple	
1 lb. spicy sausage	1 can evaporated milk	cantaloupe	
1 lb. cheddar cheese	8 oz. jalapenos or green	honeydew	

Staples:	milk	pepper	flour
	butter	eggs	
	salt	sugar	

❖ Notes ❖

Date of Gathering: _____

Guest List: _____

_____

Date of Gathering: _____

Guest List: _____

_____

Date of Gathering: _____

Guest List: _____

_____

Date of Gathering: _____

Guest List: _____

_____

Date of Gathering: _____

Guest List: _____

_____

Comments

CHAPTER FIFTEEN

✦ Hero Shower ✦

Two sweet friends Susan and Carolyn, have hosted many bridal showers together. When Carolyn's son was to be married, Susan wanted to step outside the norm and honor the groom. A "Hero Shower" evolved… and here's how it works. The bride and groom each make a list of the heroes in their life. In choosing the guest list they should consider those who have impacted them for good. For example, a soccer coach, a piano teacher or English professor, a wonderful neighbor, siblings and grandparents, aunts and uncles, church leaders; or anyone they admire. The invitation indicates the guest should share a tradition that has strengthened their marriage and life and their gift should reflect that tradition. After dinner, the crowd gathers around the gifts. As each gift is selected, the bride or groom expresses to the giver why they are a "hero" to them. The giver then explains the meaning behind the gift and shares their unique life experience. At a time when the focus is centered around the wedding couple, this shower provides a memorable means to honor each guest. It is a powerful way for the bride and groom to give back to those who have helped weave the fabric of their lives. It also creates a unique opportunity for the new couple to discover unknown details about each other and grow closer. It's a wonderful way of bringing two worlds together acquainting each other with those who have helped develop and shape the essence of who they have become!

Warning: this can turn into a long and emotional gathering!

Spinach Strawberry Pecan Salad ⚜

2 bags baby spinach

8 oz. Feta cheese

1 c. Craisins™

⅓ c. sugar

1 red onion chopped

15 strawberries sliced

2 c. sugar coated pecans

2 avocados diced

Put nuts in a frying pan, sprinkle with white sugar over low to medium heat and stir until it crystalizes. As the sugar melts it coats the nuts. Spread out on cookie sheet and let cool.

Combine salad ingredients together and chill.

Dressing:

½ c. strawberry jam

1½ c. chopped strawberries

½ c. Balsamic vinegar

Salt and Pepper

¼ c. olive oil

¼ c. water

Put all ingredients in blender, mix and serve.

Rosemary Blend ⚜

¼ c. sun dried tomatoes

1 c. heavy kosher salt

½ c. dried rosemary

1 tsp. dried red chilies

2 tbsp. coarse pepper

½ tsp. dry mustard

1 tsp. basil

1 tsp. lemon peel

2 tsp. soy oil

Preheat oven to 350°. Blend together and toss in oil and bake at 350° for 15 minutes.

Prime Rib Roast ⚜

Preheat oven to 450°. Take 6-8 lbs. boneless prime rib and rub with a generous amount of extra virgin olive oil. Heavily salt and pepper or use our Rosemary Seasoning Blend. Bake for ½ hour at 450°, then turn oven down to 325°. Roast for 15 minutes per pound. It will be perfect!

Potato Gratin ⚜

1 yellow onion, thinly sliced

2 tbsp. olive oil

2 tbsp. butter

4 lbs. russet potatoes

2 c. sliced mushrooms

2 tbsp. melted butter

¼ c. minced fresh parsley

2 c. plus 2 tbsp. heavy cream

2½ c. grated Gruyere cheese

2 tsp. kosher salt

pepper to taste

Preheat oven to 350°. Butter a 9"x 13" dish. Peel potatoes, thinly slice them. Sauté onion in olive oil and butter on medium-low heat for 15 minutes until tender. Mix the potatoes in a large bowl with 2 cups of cream, 2 cups of Gruyere cheese, salt and pepper. Add the sautéed onion and mix. Pour the potatoes into the baking dish. Slice mushrooms, coat with melted butter, and spread over the potatoes. Combine the remaining tablespoons of cream and ½ cup of Gruyere cheese and sprinkle on top. Bake for 1½ hours, until the potatoes are tender and the top is golden. Garnish with chopped parsley and allow to set for approximately 10 minutes and serve.

Candied Yams ⚜

6 large sweet potatoes/yams	2 tsp. salt	1 tsp. pepper
½ c. butter	¼ c. cream	

Preheat oven to 350°. Bake sweet potatoes in oven for 1 hour at 350°. Clean potato skins and place potato filling in bowl. Fold in butter, cream, salt and pepper, whip potatoes until creamy. Spread in 9"x 13" (or desired size) pan.

Topping:

1½ c. brown sugar	1 c. butter	1½ c. flour

Cut with pastry blender till pea size, sprinkle over sweet potatoes and bake at 350° for 15–20 minutes or until golden brown on top.

Vegetable Ribbons ⚜

3 large carrots, peeled	2 medium zucchini
2 medium yellow squash	¼ c. basil pesto (or mix to taste)
salt and pepper to taste	fresh parsley to garnish

Cut ribbon-like slices , using a vegetable peeler, from carrots, zucchini, and yellow squash. Draw the peeler lengthwise. In medium saucepan, add ½ inch of water. Heat to boiling. Add carrots, cover, and cook over medium heat for 1–2 minutes. Add zucchini and yellow squash and continue cooking 1 minute. Do not over cook to maintain crispness of vegetables. Drain well and place in serving bowl. Add pesto and season with salt and pepper to taste. Toss to coat. Garnish with fresh parsley. Serve immediately.

Toasted Pecan Pull-Apart Bread ⚜

15 frozen dinner rolls ½ c. butter

¾ c. brown sugar 1 c. chopped pecans

Using frozen dinner rolls, coat a bundt pan with non-stick cooking spray. Place frozen dough in pan and cover with plastic wrap. Let rolls rise 30min. to an hour. Cut each roll in half with scissors. Melt butter and fold in brown sugar and pecans. Roll in sugar mixture, layer in bundt pan, cover with plastic wrap, let rise 2 hours or until it raises just above bundt pan. Preheat oven to 350°. Bake rolls for 15-20 minutes. Remove from bundt.

Butter Onion Buns ⚜

15 frozen dinner rolls ½ c. butter

2 tsp. onion salt 2 tbsp. fresh chopped oregano

3 tbsp. green onions 1 tsp. salt

Using frozen dinner rolls, coat a bundt pan with non-stick cooking spray. Place frozen dough in pan and cover with plastic wrap. Let rolls rise 30min. to an hour. Cut each roll in half with scissors, melt butter, add fresh herbs and seasonings. Coat rolls in butter seasoning and place in a bundt pan, cover in plastic and let rise 2 hours or until it raises just above bundt pan. Preheat the oven to 350°. Bake rolls for 15-20 min. Remove from bundt.

Abby Jane's Eight Layer Cake

1 c. butter, softened

3 c. sugar

6 eggs

3 c. flour, sifted

1 c. heavy whipping cream

1½ tsp. almond extract

1½ c. cocoa powder

Preheat oven to 325°. Cream together butter and sugar in a mixing bowl and beat for at least 3-4 minutes. Add eggs one at a time and beat well. Add flour, cocoa powder and whipping cream, mix well. Stir in almond extract. Spoon into 2 greased 9" round cake pans (¼ of batter in each cake pan). With remaining batter fold in 2 tbsp. black food coloring. Spoon into 2 remaining greased 9 inch round cake pans. Bake at 325° for 40 minutes. Remove from oven, cover the cake pan with tin foil and cool in freezer for at least 30 minutes, so the cakes are firm enough to cut, holding shape. Remove cake from pans and take a large bread knife and slice cake through the middle creating 8 layers. Frost cake and stack alternating colors. Return to fridge until ready to serve.

Frosting:

4 c. powdered sugar

1 c. unsweetened cocoa

¾ c. butter softened

4-5 tbsp. heavy cream

1½ tsp. vanilla

Sift sugar and cocoa together in a large bowl, set aside. Whip butter until it is creamy, alternate adding sugar mixture and cream, until it is fluffy. Add vanilla and spread frosting on cake.

Hurricane Candles ⚜

Any size hurricane candleholder will work. Take a large candle and place in the bottom and surround it with fresh cranberries. These will only last about a month but you may find artificial ones at your local craft store.

❧ *Shopping List* ❧

For 10-12 people

4 c. strawberries	2 bags baby spinach	2 c. pecans	basil pesto paste
1 lemon	2 avocados	dry mustard	6-8 lbs. prime rib roast
1 yellow onion	2 bunches fresh parsley	soy oil	30 frozen dinner rolls
1 red onion	fresh oregano	dried red chilies	cocoa powder
1 bunch green onions	4 lbs. Russet potatoes	dried rosemary	unsweetened cocoa
2 c. mushrooms	8 oz. Feta cheese	basil	powdered sugar
6 large sweet potatoes/yams	2½ c. Gruyere cheese	onion salt	almond extract
3 large carrots	1 qt. heavy whipping cream	coarse pepper	1 c. Craisins™
2 medium yellow squash	balsamic vinegar	sun dried tomatoes	
2 medium zucchini	strawberry jam	heavy kosher salt	

Staples:	olive oil	butter	eggs
	salt	flour	sugar
	pepper	brown sugar	vanilla

Notes

Date of Gathering: _____

Guest List: _____
_____

Date of Gathering: _____

Guest List: _____
_____

Date of Gathering: _____

Guest List: _____
_____

Date of Gathering: _____

Guest List: _____
_____

Date of Gathering: _____

Guest List: _____
_____

❦ Comments ❦

_____

_____

_____

_____

_____

_____

_____

_____

_____

_____

_____

_____

_____

—CHAPTER SIXTEEN—

Creating a Gathering Place

When someone comes to your home, sits at your table and breaks bread with you,

your relationship is forever changed. A good friend longed to celebrate her father's

seventieth birthday in her home but felt she had no room to host such a gather-

ing. With our help she discovered that by creatively rearranging her family room she

could seat 64 people for a wonderful tribute to her father. Serving the food family

style gave the teenage grandchildren a unique opportunity to serve and participate.

The same intimacy could not have been achieved in a restaurant or rented hall.

What a splendid way to honor a beloved father.

Index

❧ Acknowledgements ❧

Thanks to our graphic designer, Kristy Witt for sharing her gifts and talents.

Thanks to Matt Christensen, our photographer we appreciate and value his expertise.

Thanks to Jim Clark and his magical way with words.

A special thanks to Abby Jane Taylor who tirelessly contributed her ideas and artistic ability to help complete this dream.

Linda Cornaby

Rachael Crittenden

Abby Jane Taylor

Heather Cornaby

Carolyn Kirkham Green

Susan Jones

Sarah Metcalf

Denise Fielding

Mary Jo Mulliner Roberts

Evelyn Bartholamew

Bonnie Clark

Gayle Peterson

Richard Bickerton

Ryan Fish

Maggie Fish

Cyd Quinn

Gay Waystaff

Debra Packard

Mrs. Benson

Shawna Benne

Hillary Stafford

Stacy Wade

Hilda Cornaby

Brayden Iwasaki

June Bickerton

Mary Rasmussen

Ali Malmrose

Pam King

Julie Anderson

Molly Welch

Dixie Philipoom

Bobette Johnson

Brooke Mason

Kathleen Johnson

Joanne Christensen

Location Credits:

Many thanks to the following for sharing their beautiful homes with us.

Kyle & Alyse Christensen

Kenneth & Michelle Huxtable

Julie Rasmussen

Jeff & Susan Jones

Rick & Denise Fielding

Vernon & Rebecca Cooley

Judd & Michelle Clawson

Michelle Huxtable has successfully created gathering places for many years as an interior designer. As a talented chef, her passion for creating a comfortable gathering place is motivated by her innate desire to surround herself and others with beauty. She feels that food is a love language and that carefully preparing a meal is a genuine expression of oneself. A creative, artistic flare embellishes everything she does. Michelle has owned an interior design firm for over 20 years and designs her own custom built furniture. She also enjoys working with her husband in the construction industry building high-end residential homes. She has six children and four grandchildren. They reside in Holladay, Utah.

Michelle Huxtable ❧ *Alyse Christensen*

Alyse Christensen graduated from the University of Utah with her Bachelor's degree in Mass Communication - Business. Born and raised in Salt Lake City, Utah, she has also lived in Vienna, Austria, The Netherlands and Seattle, Washington. She now resides in Holladay, Utah with her husband and four young children. Raised in a home where entertaining was an important part of family life, Alyse quickly learned that, no matter where she lives, she makes her home a place where friends and family gather.

Alyse and Michelle feel that when someone comes to your home and sits at your table and breaks bread with you, your relationship is forever changed.

Please visit www.thegatheringoffriends.com